视听说立体化教学设计

21世纪全国高等院校旅游管理类创新型应用人才培养规划教材

旅游英语

English for Tourism

主 编 朱 华
编 著 朱 华　李思瑶　刘 颖　王 仪
　　　　朱晓霞　赵吉明　向雨希

内 容 简 介

《旅游英语》以游客预订、离境、登机、到达目的地全过程为主线，涵盖"吃、住、行、游、购、娱"旅游六要素，涉及出境、餐饮、住宿、交通、娱乐、购物等各种旅游活动，生动有趣地再现了丰富多彩的旅游情景。教材有"旅游会话""旅行故事""旅游听力""旅游视频""旅游歌曲""旅游阅读""旅游写作"等教学模块，配置了多种互动式练习，为教师提供了电子课件，附 CD 光盘一张。

图书在版编目(CIP)数据

旅游英语/朱华主编. —北京：北京大学出版社，2014.1
(21 世纪全国高等院校旅游管理类创新型应用人才培养规划教材)
ISBN 978-7-301-23087-9

Ⅰ. ①旅… Ⅱ. ①朱… Ⅲ. ①旅游—英语—高等学校—教材 Ⅳ. ①H31

中国版本图书馆 CIP 数据核字(2013)第 199110 号

书　　　名：旅游英语
著作责任者：朱　华　主编
策　划　编　辑：莫　愚
责　任　编　辑：莫　愚
标　准　书　号：ISBN 978-7-301-23087-9/C · 0932
出　版　发　行：北京大学出版社
地　　　址：北京市海淀区成府路 205 号　100871
网　　　址：http://www.pup.cn　新浪官方微博：@北京大学出版社
电　子　信　箱：pup_6@163.com
电　　　话：邮购部 62752015　　发行部 62750672　　编辑部 62750667　　出版部 62754962
印　刷　者：北京富生印刷厂
经　销　者：新华书店
　　　　　　787 毫米×1092 毫米　16 开本　17.5 印张　420 千字
　　　　　　2014 年 1 月第 1 版　2020 年 8 月第 7 次印刷
定　　　价：48.00 元 (含 1CD)

未经许可，不得以任何方式复制或抄袭本书之部分或全部内容。
版权所有，侵权必究
举报电话：010-62752024　电子信箱：fd@pup.pku.edu.cn

前言

《旅游英语》以游客预订、离境、登机、到达目的地全过程为主线，涵盖"吃、住、行、游、购、娱"旅游六要素，涉及出境、餐饮、住宿、交通、娱乐、购物等各种旅游活动，生动有趣地再现了丰富多彩的旅游情景。

教材设计有"旅游会话""旅行故事""旅游听力""旅游视频""旅游歌曲""旅游阅读""旅游写作"等教学模块，有多种互动式练习，为教师提供电子课件，附CD光盘一张，任课教师可在www.pup6.com下载课件，或致函ernestzhu@126索取。

由于学生英语水平层次不同，建议课时分配如下：

教学内容	课时分配		
	专科	本科	培训
	54	36	66
第1章 预订机票 Reservation for Air Tickets	3	2	4
第2章 机场登机 Airport Check-in	3	2	4
第3章 飞行途中 On the Flight	3	2	4
第4章 抵达机场 Landing at the Airport	3	2	4
第5章 旅游交通 Tourism Transportation	4	2	4
第6章 入住酒店 Hotel Check-in	3	2	4
第7章 退房结账 Hotel Check-out	3	2	4
第8章 主题公园 Theme Parks	3	2	4
第9章 聚会派对 Get-togethers	3	2	4
第10章 餐饮酒水 Foods and Drinks	4	2	4
第11章 付账买单 Footing the Bill	3	2	4
第12章 邮轮旅游 Cruise Travel	3	2	4
第13章 国外旅游 Travel Abroad	3	2	4
第14章 旅游购物 Shopping	3	2	4
第15章 突发事件 Emergencies	4	3	4
第16章 投诉处理 Complaint Settlement	4	3	4
总复习	2	2	2

朱 华

2013年8月

Contents
目 录

Chapter 1　Reservation for Air Tickets 预订机票

旅游会话 Speaking for Travel	3
旅游听力 Listening for Travel	5
旅游视频 Watching for Travel	6
旅游阅读 Reading for Travel	7
旅游歌曲 Singing for Travel	10
知识扩展 Additional Know-how	11

Chapter 2　Airport Check-in 机场登机

旅游会话 Speaking for Travel	15
旅游听力 Listening for Travel	17
旅游视频 Watching for Travel	18
旅游阅读 Reading for Travel	20
旅游写作 Writing for Travel	22
旅游歌曲 Singing for Travel	24
知识扩展 Additional Know-how	25

Chapter 3　On the Flight 飞行途中

旅游会话 Speaking for Travel	29
旅游听力 Listening for Travel	31

旅游视频 Watching for Travel	32
旅游阅读 Reading for Travel	33
旅游歌曲 Singing for Travel	36
知识扩展 Additional Know-how	37

Chapter 4　Landing at the Airport 抵达机场

旅游会话 Speaking for Travel	41
旅游听力 Listening for Travel	43
旅游视频 Watching for Travel	44
旅游阅读 Reading for Travel	46
旅游写作 Writing for Travel	49
旅游歌曲 Singing for Travel	50
知识扩展 Additional Know-how	51

Chapter 5　Tourism Transportation 旅游交通

旅游会话 Speaking for Travel	55
旅游听力 Listening for Travel	57
旅游视频 Watching for Travel	58
旅游阅读 Reading for Travel	60
旅游歌曲 Singing for Travel	62
知识扩展 Additional Know-how	63

Chapter 6　Hotel Check-in 入住酒店

旅游会话 Speaking for Travel	67
旅游听力 Listening for Travel	69
旅游视频 Watching for Travel	70
旅游阅读 Reading for Travel	71
旅游写作 Writing for Travel	74

	旅游歌曲 Singing for Travel	76
	知识扩展 Additional Know-how	77

Chapter 7 Hotel Check-out 退房结账

	旅游会话 Speaking for Travel	81
	旅游听力 Listening for Travel	83
	旅游视频 Watching for Travel	84
	旅游阅读 Reading for Travel	86
	旅游歌曲 Singing for Travel	89
	知识扩展 Additional Know-how	91

Chapter 8 Theme Parks 主题公园

	旅游会话 Speaking for Travel	95
	旅游听力 Listening for Travel	97
	旅游视频 Watching for Travel	98
	旅游阅读 Reading for Travel	99
	旅游写作 Writing for Travel	101
	旅游歌曲 Singing for Travel	103
	知识扩展 Additional Know-how	105

Chapter 9 Get-together 聚会派对

	旅游会话 Speaking for Travel	109
	旅游听力 Listening for Travel	111
	旅游视频 Watching for Travel	112
	旅游阅读 Reading for Travel	113
	旅游歌曲 Singing for Travel	116
	知识扩展 Additional Know-how	117

Chapter 10   Foods and Drinks 餐饮酒水

旅游会话 Speaking for Travel	121
旅游听力 Listening for Travel	123
旅游视频 Watching for Travel	124
旅游阅读 Reading for Travel	125
旅游写作 Writing for Travel	128
旅游歌曲 Singing for Travel	129
知识扩展 Additional Know-how	130

Chapter 11   Footing the Bill 付账买单

旅游会话 Speaking for Travel	135
旅游听力 Listening for Travel	137
旅游视频 Watching for Travel	138
旅游阅读 Reading for Travel	140
旅游歌曲 Singing for Travel	143
知识扩展 Additional Know-how	145

Chapter 12   Cruise Travel 邮轮旅游

旅游会话 Speaking for Travel	149
旅游听力 Listening for Travel	151
旅游视频 Watching for Travel	152
旅游阅读 Reading for Travel	153
旅游写作 Writing for Travel	156
旅游歌曲 Singing for Travel	158
知识扩展 Additional Know-how	159

Chapter 13　Travel Abroad 国外旅游

旅游会话 Speaking for Travel	163
旅游听力 Listening for Travel	165
旅游视频 Watching for Travel	166
旅游阅读 Reading for Travel	167
旅游歌曲 Singing for Travel	171
知识扩展 Additional Know-how	172

Chapter 14　Shopping 旅游购物

旅游会话 Speaking for Travel	177
旅游听力 Listening for Travel	179
旅游视频 Watching for Travel	180
旅游阅读 Reading for Travel	181
旅游写作 Writing for Travel	184
旅游歌曲 Singing for Travel	186
知识扩展 Additional Know-how	187

Chapter 15　Emergencies 突发事件

旅游会话 Speaking for Travel	191
旅游听力 Listening for Travel	193
旅游视频 Watching for Travel	194
旅游阅读 Reading for Travel	195
旅游歌曲 Singing for Travel	198
知识扩展 Additional Know-how	199

Chapter 16　Complaint Settlement 投诉处理

旅游会话 Speaking for Travel	203

旅游听力 Listening for Travel	205
旅游视频 Watching for Travel	206
旅游阅读 Reading for Travel	207
旅游写作 Writing for Travel	209
旅游歌曲 Singing for Travel	211
知识扩展 Additional Know-how	212

Reference Keys 参考答案   214

References   参考文献   266

Chapter 1

Reservation for Air Tickets
预订机票

Focus on Learning 学习要点

- 旅游会话　　Flight Reconfirmation 航班再确认
- 旅行故事　　I Know It's a Big Animal 我知道它是个大动物
- 旅游听力　　E-Ticket 电子机票
- 旅游视频　　How to Save Money to Book Air Tickets? 如何省钱订机票？
- 旅游阅读　　Airline Reservations 机票预订
- 旅游歌曲　　Take Me Home, Country Road 乡村路带我回家
- 知识扩展　　Travel Agency 旅行社

Useful Words and Expressions

retail(零售)/ˈriːteil/: the sale of goods to ultimate consumers, usually in small quantities

devote to(致力于，专心): give up (oneself, one's time, energy, etc.) to

specialize in(专攻，专门研究): give special or particular attention to

commercial(商业的) /kəˈməːʃəl/: of or for commerce

headquarters(总部，司令部) /ˌhedˈkwɔːtə/: place from which(e.g. police or army) operations are controlled

discount(折扣) /ˈdiskaunt/: amount of money which may be taken off the full price, e.g. of goods bought by shopkeepers for resale of an account if paid promptly, of a bill of exchange not yet due for payment

commission(佣金) /kəˈmiʃən/: payment for sb. for selling goods etc. rising in proportion to the results gained

reservation(预定) /ˌrezəˈveiʃən/: travel arrangement to keep sth. for sb. e.g. a seat in a train or aircraft, a passage on a ship, a room in a hotel

electronic(电子的) /ilekˈtrɔnik/: of electrons, operated by, based on electrons

virtually(事实上) /ˈvɜːtjuəli/: being in fact, acting as, what is described, but not accepted openly

assign(分派) /əˈsain/: give for use or enjoyment or as a share or part in distribution e.g. of work, duty

departure(出发) / diˈpɑːtʃə/: an act of leaving

boarding pass(登机牌): a pass that authorizes a passenger to board an aircraft and is issued after one's ticket has been purchased or collected

eliminate(除去，剔除) /iˈlimineit/: remove, take or put away, get rid of

Chapter 1 Reservation for Air Tickets 预订机票

Speaking for Travel
旅游会话

I. Dialogue

Flight Reconfirmation 航班再确认

1. Listen to the situational dialogue carefully, and match the information in column A with that in column B.

Column A	Column B
1) reason for calling	A. Orlando, Florida
2) flight number	B. 11:43 pm
3) leaving date	C. to reconfirm the flight
4) destination	D. May 11th
5) local time when arriving	E. 1079

2. Listen to the situational dialogue again, repeat it sentence by sentence, and then role play it in pairs.

Clerk: United Airline, can I help you?

Peter: Hello, I'd like to reconfirm my flight, please.

Clerk: May I have your name and flight number, please?

Peter: My name is Peter, Peter Wilson, and my flight number is 1079.

Clerk: When are you leaving?

Peter: On May 11th.

Clerk: And your destination?

Peter: Orlando, Florida.

English for Tourism

Clerk: Hold the line, please. (...) All right. Your seat is confirmed, Mr. Wilson. You will be arriving in Orlando, Florida at 11:43 p.m. local time.

Peter: Thank you. Can I pick up the ticket when I check in?

Clerk: Yes, but please check in at least one hour before departure time.

Peter: OK. Thank you, and have a nice day!

II. Story—retelling

Listen to the funny story and retell it using your own words. You may refer to the key words or phrases given in the box.

| Hippopotamus | was at a loss | flight | searching | looked up |
| airport code | retorted | scoured | offered | Buffalo |

I Know It's a Big Animal 我知道它是个大动物

A woman called to make reservations, "I want to go from Chicago to Hippopotamus, New York." The agent was at a loss for words. Finally, the agent asked, "Are you sure that's the name of the town?"

"Yes, what flights do you have?" replied the customer. After some searching, the agent came back and said, "I'm sorry, ma'am, I've looked up every airport code in the country and can't find a Hippopotamus anywhere."

The customer retorted, "Oh don't be silly. Everyone knows where it is. Check your map!" The agent scoured a map of the state of New York and finally offered, "You don't mean Buffalo, do you?"

"That's it! I knew it's a big animal!"

Chapter 1 Reservation for Air Tickets 预订机票

Listening for Travel 旅游听力

E-Ticket 电子机票

1. Listen to the passage twice and fill in the blanks with the information you hear (one word for one blank).

An e-ticket is a 1)_____ electronic document used for ticketing passengers, particularly in the commercial airline industry. Virtually all major airlines now use this method of ticketing.

When a customer books a 2)_____ by telephone or using the Web, the details of the reservation are stored in a computer. The customer can request that a 3)_____ confirmation be sent by postal mail, but it is not needed at the check-in desk. A confirmation number is 4)_____ to the passenger, along with the flight number, date, 5)_____ location, and destination location. When checking in at the airport, the passenger simply presents positive 6)_____. Then necessary boarding passes are issued, and the passenger can check luggage and proceed through 7)_____ to the gate area.

The 8)_____ advantage of e-ticketing is the fact that it reduces booking 9)_____ by eliminating the need for printing and mailing paper documents. Another advantage is that it eliminates the possibility of 10)_____ documents getting lost in the mail or being sent to the wrong address.

2. Orally summarize the main ideas of the above passage and write them down on the following lines.

1) _____
2) _____
3) _____

English for Tourism

Watching for Travel
旅游视频

How to Save Money to Book Air Tickets? 如何省钱订机票？

Brief information from the video:

Consider Flying in Off-Peak Times: Flexibility is the key to an inexpensive getaway. Discounts can be found during off-peak times and seasons.

Try Flying into Nearby Airports: Once you pick a city, consider flying into nearby airports. Sometimes you can save a bundle arriving into one airport and leaving from another.

Be Flexible with Travel Dates: Research is essential to save your money. There are gobs of great online tools to help you find the lowest fare. Some even send you alerts when prices drop between your favorite cities.

Buy Direct from the Airline: Although these travel sites are great, they charge a service fee of at least $5 when it's time to book. Don't even think about calling an airline to buy a ticket unless you absolutely have to. They all charge fees to talk with someone, in hopes you'll complete your purchase on the Internet.

Know When to Book Your Flight: The best time to book your tickets may be mid-week. Airlines usually announce fare sales around Wednesday or Thursday, and hike fares on the weekend. If you need to book at the last second, forget this and snag the best price you can find as soon as possible.

Sign Up for E-mail Alerts: Speaking of last minute tickets, you can find impressive bargains when booking just before take-off. The airlines offer e-mail blasts once a week. And every penny you save getting there is one you can spend once you arrive. Thanks for watching.

Chapter 1 Reservation for Air Tickets 预订机票

Watch the short video twice, and complete the following requirements.

Step 1: Divide the class into groups, and ask each student to take a note of what they have watched or heard. Compare the notes with their teammates.

Step 2: Make a brief summary of ways to save money when booking air tickets according to the video.

Summary:
1) _____
2) _____
3) _____

Reading for Travel 旅游阅读

Airline Reservations 机票预订

1. Listen to the passage and decide whether the following statements are true or false. Write T for true and F for false.

With the explosion of the Internet, calling the airline reservation desk to book a flight is no longer necessary—in fact, it may cost you. Many airlines are now charging fees to book through a phone representative, encouraging customers to go online, either directly to the airline's website, or to the many airline ticket comparison and booking sites on the web. No matter how you decide to reserve your ticket, browsing the Internet for tickets before you book can save you money.

Identify the specific flight you want. No matter which method you choose to reserve or book your tickets, the process will go faster and be cheaper if you know the exact flight information. By using the Internet to find your ticket, you can save a considerable amount of money. Start on a site such as KAYAK.com,

FareCompare.com or priceline.com. With these sites you can compare all airlines that fly to your destination simply by entering your desired departure and arrival information.

Once you've found a ticket at the time and price you want, don't reserve it just yet. Visit Farecast.live.com, a site that not only compares ticket prices, but also makes predictions about whether ticket prices will fall or rise before your departure. Enter your departure and arrival information to get Farecast's advice on whether to purchase/reserve your ticket now or wait.

Visit the airline's website directly. Here you will find specific information about reserving the ticket you want. If you choose to reserve your ticket over the phone, you can visit the airline's website to find out if there is an extra charge to do so.

Check the terms and conditions of your ticket reservation. This is also something that can be done on the website of the airline from which you decide to purchase your ticket. This information will tell you if you can change or cancel your ticket, and if penalties or charges will apply in this situation.

When ready to book your flight, use the airline's website or reservation desk (by phone) to do so, rather than using a third-party site or agent. Booking on the airline's website will typically save you money over using price comparison sites or travel agents, as both typically charge additional booking fees.

1) _____ Many airlines now encourage customers to go online directly to their own websites to book the ticket.

2) _____ Reserve the ticket once you've found a ticket at the time and price you want.

3) _____ Sites such as SideStep.com or Priceline.com can let you compare ticket price to your destination by entering your departure and arrival information.

4) _____ FareCompare.com can not only let you compare ticket price but also predict the rising or falling of the ticket price before your departure.

Chapter 1 Reservation for Air Tickets 预订机票

5) _____ You'd better make sure whether there would be an extra charge for booking the ticket over the phone.

6) _____ Booking on the airline's website and booking through travel agents both typically charge additional booking fees.

> **Word Tips**
> explosion:　　剧增　　　　reservation:　　预订　　　browse:　浏览
> prediction:　　预测　　　　penalty:　　　　惩罚

2. Discuss: What are the advantages of booking air tickets online?

With the wonders of technology and the creation of the world-wide-web, the world seems to be a smaller place than before and life has become simpler; booking plane tickets has never been so easy before. If you are one of those who still think that booking airline tickets is a tough task, you have to take some time in finding out how easy and how great it is to get good flight deals online.

Lead-in Questions:

1) Do you think booking air tickets online is a convenient way?

2) In what way do you think it is convenient?

3) How do you understand that security is another advantage when booking air tickets online?

4) In what way can booking online help you to save money?

5) How do you understand that booking air tickets online is a time-saving way?

Group Work: What are the advantages of booking air tickets online?

Step 1: Divide the class into groups.

Step 2: Ask students to discuss in details the above questions and summarize.

Step 3: Have some groups give their presentations in front of the class.

English for Tourism

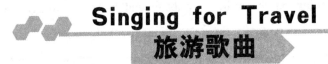

Singing for Travel 旅游歌曲

Take Me Home, Country Road 乡村路带我回家

John Denver

1. Singing English songs together with tourists can stimulate their interest, and liven up the atmosphere when they travel. Listen to the song casually with reference to the lyrics.

Almost heaven
West Virginia
Blue Ridge Mountain
Shenandoah River
Life is old there
Older than the trees
Younger than the mountains
Growing like a breeze

Country road. take me home
To the place I belong
West Virginia
Mountain Mama
Take me home, country roads
All my memories
Gather round her
Miner's Lady
Stranger to blue water
Dark and dusty
Painted on the sky

Misty taste of moonshine
Teardrops in my eyes

Country roads, take me home
To the place I belong
West Virginia
Mountain Mama
Take me home, country roads

I hear her voice in the morning hours
She calls me
The radio reminds me of my home far away
And driving down the road
I get a feeling
That I should have been home
Yesterday, yesterday

Country roads , take me home
To the place I belong
West Virginia

Chapter 1　Reservation for Air Tickets 预订机票

Mountain Mama
Take me home, country roads

West Virginia
Mountain Mama
Take me home, country roads

Country roads, take me home
To the place I belong

Take me home, country roads
Take me home, country roads

2. One student role plays a tour guide while others act as tourists. Sing and enjoy the English song together.

Additional Know-how 知识扩展

Travel Agency 旅行社

A travel agency is a retail business, selling travel related products and services to customers. It represents suppliers, such as airlines, car rentals, cruise lines, hotels, railways, sightseeing tours and package holidays. In addition to dealing with ordinary tourists, most travel agencies have a separate department devoted to making travel arrangements for business travelers. Some specialize in commercial and business travel only. Some serve as general sales agents for foreign travel companies, allowing them to have branch offices in different countries from their headquarters.

The British company, Cox & Kings, is said to be the oldest travel agency in the world. Modern travel agencies begin with Thomas Cook in the late 19th century. Brownell Travel established in 1887 is the oldest one in North America. With the development of commercial aviation from the 1920s, travel agencies become more popular.

As the name implies, a travel agency's main function is to act as an agent. Its profit is the difference between the advertised price paid by customers and the discounted price provided by suppliers. This is known as the commission. A British travel agent would consider a 10%-12% commission as a good arrangement. In the United States, most airlines pay no commission at all to travel agencies. Travel agencies, in this case, usually add a service fee to the net price.

Reservation through travel agencies is a traditional way. Since the process of planning your trips and looking forward to new adventures is an exciting experience, finding a travel agent that meets your needs will help to make your dreams come true.

Read the passage aloud, and decide whether the following statements are true or false. Write T for true and F for false.

1) _____ A travel agency is a retail business, dealing with ordinary tourists, but not business travelers.

2) _____ Some travel agencies serve as general sales agents for foreign travel companies, allowing the existence of branch office in different countries.

3) _____ The American company, Cox & Kings, is said to be the oldest travel agency in the world.

4) _____ The commission of travel agencies is the difference between the advertised price paid by customers and the discounted price provided by suppliers.

5) _____ In the United States, most airlines pay no commission at all to travel agencies.

Chapter 2

Airport Check-in
机场登机

→ Focus on Learning 学习要点

- 旅游会话　　Weight Limit 行李限重
- 旅行故事　　Kissing the Luggage Goodbye 与行李吻别
- 旅游听力　　Online Check-in 网上检票
- 旅游视频　　How to Get to the Airport on Time?
　　　　　　如何按时到达机场?
- 旅游阅读　　Expressions Related to Air Travel 航空旅游相关表述
- 旅游写作　　Customs Declaration Form 海关申报表
- 旅游歌曲　　Big Big World 大千世界
- 知识扩展　　ABC about Airport Check-in 机场登机常识

Useful Words and Expressions

handle(处理)/ˈhændl/: to manage, deal with, or be responsible for

on behalf of(代表): as a representative of or a proxy for

domestic(国内的)/dəˈmestik/: of or pertaining to one's own or a particular country as apart from other countries

prior to(在……之前): before

inquire(询问)/inˈkwaiə/: to seek information by questioning; ask

upgrade(给……升级)/ˈʌpgreid/: to promote to a higher grade or rank

overweight(超重的)/ˈəuvəweit/: weighing more than is considered normal, proper, etc.

proceed(继续进行)/prəˈsi:d/: to go on to do something

inspect(检查)/inˈspekt/: to look carefully at or over; view closely and critically

stamp(把……印盖在)/stæmp/: to impress with a particular mark or device, as to indicate genuineness, approval, or ownership

lounge(休息室)/laundʒ/: a place for sitting, waiting, smoking, etc., esp. a large public room, as in a hotel, theater, or air terminal, often with adjoining washrooms

procedure(步骤)/prəˈsi:dʒə/: a particular course or mode of action

abide by(遵守): to act in accord with

ample(充足的)/ˈæmpl/: fully sufficient or more than adequate for the purpose or needs; plentiful; enough

option(选择)/ˈɔpʃən/: something that may be or is chosen; choice

Chapter 2 Airport Check-in 机场登机

Speaking for Travel 旅游会话

I. Dialogue

Weight Limit 行李限重

1. Listen to the situational dialogue carefully, and match the information in column A with that in column B.

Column A	Column B
1) flight number	A. only one
2) destination	B. economy
3) class	C. 40 lb
4) weight limit	D. UA856
5) number of bags	E. Los Angeles

2. Listen to the situational dialogue again, repeat it sentence by sentence, and then role play it in pairs.

Staff:　Good morning. Can I help you?

Bob:　Good morning. I'd like to check in for UA 856 to Los Angeles.

Staff:　Your passport and ticket, please?

Bob:　Here you are. Can I have a window seat?

Staff:　Certainly. How many bags do you have?

Bob:　Only one.

Staff:　Would you please put it on the scale?

Bob:　All right. What is the weight limit?

English for Tourism

Staff: Well, it depends on the class of your ticket. What class are you traveling?

Bob: Economy class.

Staff: 40 lb.

Bob: I hope my baggage isn't overweight.

Staff: No, it isn't. Here are your boarding pass and baggage claim ticket. Have a good trip!

Bob: Thank you!

II. Story-retelling

Listen to the funny story and retell it using your own words. You may refer to the key words or phrases given in the box.

Christmas	decorate	blare	annoying
take…seriously	mood	mistletoe	Picasso sort of way
irritation	vent	luggage scale	

Kissing the Luggage Goodbye 与行李吻别

It was a few days before Christmas. The trip went reasonably well, and the traveller was ready to go back home. The airport had been decorated red and green, and the loudspeakers blared annoying renditions of cherished Christmas carols.

Being someone who took Christmas very seriously, and being slightly tired, he was not in a particularly good mood. Going to check in his luggage, he saw hanging mistletoe. Not real mistletoe, but very cheap plastic with red paint on some of the rounder parts and green paint on some of the flatter and pointer parts, that could be taken for mistletoe only in a very Picasso sort of way.

With a considerable degree of irritation and nowhere else to vent it, he said to the attendant, "Even if we were married, I would not want to kiss you under such a ghastly mockery of mistletoe."

Chapter 2 Airport Check-in 机场登机

"Sir, look more closely at where the mistletoe is."

"Ok, I see that it's above the luggage scale which is the place you'd have to step forward for a kiss."

"That's not why it's there."

"Ok, I give up. Why is it there?"

"It's there so you can kiss your luggage good-bye."

Listening for Travel 旅游听力

Online Check-in 网上检票

1. Listen to the passage twice and fill in the blanks with the information you hear (one word for one blank).

Online check-in is the process where passengers 1)_____ their presence on a flight via the internet, and typically print their own 2)_____ passes. Depending on the carrier and the 3)_____ flight, passengers may also enter details such as meal options and baggage quantities and select their 4)_____ seating.

This service is generally 5)_____ by the airlines to passengers as being easier and faster because it avoids the need to queue at the airport 6)_____ counter; furthermore, online check-in for a flight is often 7)_____ earlier than its in-person counterpart. Typically, web based check-in for airline travel is offered on the airline's website not earlier than 24 hours before a flight's 8)_____ departure or 7 days for Internet Check-In Assistant. However, some airlines allow a longer time, such as Ryanair which

English for Tourism

opens online check-in 5 days beforehand. Depending on the airline, there can be 9)_____ of better seating or upgrades to first/business class offered to the first people to check-in for a flight. In order to meet this demand, some sites have offered travelers the ability to 10)_____ an airline check-in prior to the 24-hour window and receive airline boarding passes by email.

2. Orally summarize the main ideas of the above passage and write them down on the following lines.

1) _____
2) _____
3) _____

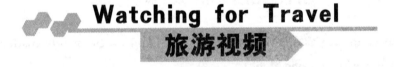

How to Get to the Airport on Time? 如何按时到达机场?

Brief information from the video:

Catching a flight is tricky. Leave too early and you'll sit at the gate for hours; leave too late and you might miss your plane.

Confirm your departure time the morning of or the night before your flight, either by calling your airline or checking online.

Visit the Transportation Security Administration's website at www.tsa.gov for security waiting times at all the major airports. Sign up for updates from your airline's website.

Listen to the radio traffic report for accidents and construction projects that might slow you down and budget your time accordingly.

Chapter 2　Airport Check-in 机场登机

If you're leaving your car at the airport, visit the airport's website to find out exactly where long-term and short-term parking is located. Also, map the best route online. Research the best way to get from the parking lot to the main terminal.

If you're getting a ride with a service or even a friend, confirm when and where the driver is picking you up. If you're taking the bus, double-check the schedule.

If you're taking a cab, leave plenty of time to catch one—especially in the rain.

If you're headed to a big airport, call on your way to confirm that your departure gate and check-in terminal hasn't changed.

When you arrive, have your ticket and ID out. It will help you get through check-in faster.

Watch the short video twice, and complete the following requirements.

Step 1: Divide the class into groups, and ask each student to take a note of what they have watched or heard. Compare the notes with their teammates.

Step 2: Make a brief summary of ways to get to the airport on time according to the video.

Summary:

1) _____

_____

2) _____

_____

3) _____

_____

4) _____

_____

5) _____

_____

English for Tourism

Reading for Travel
旅游阅读

Expressions Related to Air Travel 航空旅游相关表述

1. Survey: Take this quiz to find out how much you know about expressions related to air travel. Words in the following box are for your reference.

baggage claim	gate	carry-on	baggage
aisle seat	window seat	seat assignment	visa
check in	passport	ticket	reservation
flight number	domestic	international	flight
customs	boarding pass	claim check	

1) Document which identifies you as a citizen of a certain country and which allows you to travel to other countries is called a _____.

2) A flight within one country is called a _____ flight.

3) A flight between different countries is called a(n) _____ flight.

4) The letters and numbers which identify an airplane making a specific flight are called a _____.

5) The section of an airport, station, etc., where baggage is checked for contraband and for goods subject to duty is called _____.

6) A printed piece of paper which allows you to travel on an airplane is a _____.

7) The first thing to do at the airport is _____, which means to register as a passenger for a flight.

8) A trip on an airplane is called a _____.

Chapter 2   Airport Check-in 机场登机

9) A small ticket with printed numbers that identify your baggage is called a baggage _____.

10) Ordering a seat to be held for you on the day you want to travel is called making a _____.

11) The selection of a specific seat for a trip on an airplane is called _____.

12) A seat next to the window in an airplane is called a _____.

13) A seat next to the passage between the rows of seats in an airplane is called an _____.

14) The suitcases and bags which contain your belongings are called _____.

15) The area where you pick up your baggage after a flight is called _____.

16) Stamp in your passport which allows you to travel to another country is called a _____.

17) A printed card which allows you to get on an airplane is called a _____.

18) A door which leads from the airport building into an airplane is called a _____.

19) A bag which you carry with on the airplane is called a _____ bag.

Word Tips

identify:	认出	specific:	特定的
register:	登记	document:	证件
contraband:	违禁品	passage:	通道
contain:	容纳	belongings:	财物

2. Discuss: What do you need to do before and after arriving at the airport?

Compared with other means of transportation, traveling by air is more convenient and comfortable. And now more and more people choose this way to

21

travel. However, there are also some troubles, such as the long time spent on check-in. Therefore, it is necessary to make some preparations to ensure a smooth travel experience.

Lead-in Questions:

1) What travel documents should you bring with?

2) When will you leave for the airport?

3) How do you know you haven't forgotten anything necessary for the trip?

4) What is the first thing you should do at the airport?

5) If you find there is a long queue in front of the check-in counter, what will you do?

Group Work: What do you need to do before and after arriving at the airport?

Step 1: Divide the class into groups.

Step 2: Ask students to discuss in details what they need to do before and after arriving at the airport.

Step 3: Have some groups give their presentations in front of the class.

Customs Declaration Form 海关申报表

Fill in the Customs Declaration Form and present it to the Customs officials. Make a dialogue between the tourist and the Customs officials.

Chapter 2 Airport Check-in 机场登机

Customs Declaration Form

NAME _____

NATIONALITY _____ PASSPORT NO. _____

FROM /TO _____

NUMBER OF ACCOMPANYING CHILDREN UNDRER 16 _____

HAND BAGGAGE _____Pcs. CHECKED BAGGAGE _____Pcs.

ITEM		ENTRY		EXIT	
CHINESE & FOREIGN CURRENCIES		Description & Amount			
GOLD & SILVER ORNAMENTS					
TRIP NECESSITIES		BRAND	PEICE	BRAND	PIECE
CAMERA					
TAPE RECORDER					
VIDEO & MOVE CAMERA					
OTHER ARTICLES DUE TO CUSTOM PROCEDURES					
GOODS & SAMPLES	Yes/ No		☐	Yes /No	☐
RECORDED VIDEO TAPE	Yes / No		☐	Yes / No	☐
PRINTED MATTER	Yes / No		☐	Yes / No	☐
ANTIQUES	Yes / No		☐	Yes / No	☐
DURABLE CONSUMER GOODS (PRICE≥￥50.00) AND GIFTS (TOTAL PRICE ≥￥50.00)					
DESCRIPTION	BRAND		PIECE	CUSTOMS REMARK	

IN ADDITION ____PIECES OF UNACCOMPANIED BAGGAGE ARE TO BE IMPORTED THROUGH ____WITHIN 3 MONTHS.

SIGNTURE:_____ DATE:_____

CUSTOMS REMARDS:

Singing for Travel 旅游歌曲

Big Big World 大千世界

Emilia

1. Singing English songs together with tourists can stimulate their interest, and liven up the atmosphere when they travel. Listen to the song casually with reference to the lyrics.

I'm a big big girl

In a big big world

It's not a big big thing if you leave me

But I do do feel

That I do do will miss you much

Miss you much

I can see the first leaf falling

It's all yellow and nice

It's so very cold outside

Like the way I'm feeling inside

I'm a big big girl

In a big big world

It's not a big big thing if you leave me

But I do do feel

That I do do will miss you much

Miss you much

Outside it's now raining

And tears are falling from my eyes

Why did it have to happen

Why did it all have to end

I'm a big big girl

In a big big world

It's not a big big thing if you leave me

But I do do feel

That I do do will miss you much

Miss you much

I have your arms around me like fire

But when I open my eyes

You're gone

I'm a big big girl

Chapter 2 Airport Check-in 机场登机

In a big big world	I'm a big big girl
It's not a big big thing if you leave me	In a big big world
But I do do feel	It's not a big big thing if you leave me
That I do do will miss you much	But I do feel I will miss you much
Miss you much	Miss you much

2. One student role plays a tour guide while others act as tourists. Sing and enjoy the English song together.

Additional Know-how 知识扩展

ABC about Airport Check-in 机场登机常识

    Airport check-in is a service found at commercial airports dealing with commercial air travel. The check-in is normally handled by an airline or a handling agent on behalf of an airline.

    Check-in at the right counter is the first thing you need to do when arriving at the airport. Although different airlines may have different regulations as to the time of check-in, generally, for an international travel, you'd better arrive and check in at least 2 hours before the scheduled departure time; and for a domestic travel, you should arrive at least thirty minutes prior to the departure. While checking in, you should show your ticket, ID card, or passport and visa. Meanwhile, you can enjoy such services as choosing seats, inquiring about flight or destination information, or paying for upgrades and so on.

    If necessary, you can also check in your baggage. The baggage you are allowed to take should be within the weight limit; otherwise, you will have to pay overweight charge, which is usually very high. After getting the boarding pass and paying the airport tax (if it is not included in the ticket), you should proceed to the boarding gate, having your documents inspected and stamped and going through security inspection. Then, you can have a good rest in the lounge until your flight is called.

Occasionally different airline may have different check-in procedures with some airlines allowing certain restrictions. Sometimes even the same airline at two separate airports may also have different check-in procedures. When one carrier refuses to abide by the procedure that another carrier normally would be willing to do, it will lead to service interruption to passengers. So you'd better leave ample time for check-in.

Read the passage aloud, and decide whether the following statements are true or false. Write T for true and F for false.

1) _____ When you arrive at the airport, the first thing you need to do is check-in.

2) _____ If you are taking a domestic travel, you need to arrive at the airport at least 2 hours before the scheduled departure time.

3) _____ You can enjoy such services as choosing seats, inquiring about flight or destination information, or paying for upgrades while checking in.

4) _____ The overweight charge for baggage is not too high.

5) _____ The same airline at two separate airports always has similar check-in procedures.

Chapter 3

On the Flight
飞行途中

Focus on Learning 学习要点

- 旅游会话　　In-flight TV Programs and Channels
　　　　　　　机上电视节目和频道
- 旅行故事　　The Plane is Crashing into the Ocean
　　　　　　　飞机要掉到海里啦
- 旅游听力　　Useful Tips Onboard 机上有用小贴士
- 旅游视频　　How to Recover from Jet Lag? 怎样倒时差?
- 旅游阅读　　Are Blind Pilots Flying? 盲人飞行员在飞吗?
- 旅游歌曲　　Take Me To Your Heart 把我带进你的心
- 知识扩展　　In-flight Services 机上服务

Useful Words and Expressions

exotic(异国情调的)/ɪgˈzɔtik/: of foreign origin or character; not native; introduced from abroad, but not fully naturalized or acclimatized

long-haul(长途运输的): (esp. of an aircraft flight) covering a long distance around the world

turbulence(湍流)/ˈtɜːbjʊləns/: irregular motion of the atmosphere, as that indicated by gusts and lulls in the wind

category(类别)/ˈkætigəri/: any general or comprehensive division; a class

advanced(高级的)/ədˈvɑːnst/: ahead or far or further along in progress, complexity, knowledge, skill, etc.

entertainment(娱乐)/entəˈteinmənt/: something affording pleasure, diversion, or amusement, esp. a performance of some kind

install(安装)/inˈstɔːl/: to place in position or connect for service or use

various(各种各样的)/ˈvɛəriəs/: of different kinds, as two or more things; differing one from another

complimentary(免费赠送的)/ˌkɔmpliˈment(ə)ri/: given free as a gift or courtesy

headset(耳机)/ˈhedset/: earphones or headphones

assorted(各种各样混杂在一起的)/əˈsɔːtɪd/: consisting of different or various kinds; miscellaneous

formality(正式手续)/fɔːˈmæliti/: accordance with required or traditional rules, procedures, etc.

Chapter 3　On the Flight 飞行途中

Speaking for Travel 旅游会话

I. Dialogue

In-flight TV Programs and Channels 机上电视节目和频道

1. Listen to the situational dialogue carefully, and match the information in column A with that in column B.

Column A	Column B
1) reason for calling	A. channel 9
2) discovery channel	B. a glass of grape juice with ice
3) music channel	C. channels 6 to 8
4) heavy metal	D. want help to find a war movie
5) beverage required	E. channels 9 to 12

2. Listen to the situational dialogue again, repeat it sentence by sentence, and then role play it in pairs.

John: Flight attendant.

F.A.: Yes, sir. What can I do for you?

John: I'd like to watch a war movie. Could you tell me which channel the movie is on?

F.A.: OK. Let me see. Channels 1 to 3 offer programs provided by NBC. 4 to 5 are Disney Channels and 6 to 8 are discovery channels. I think you'd better browse through these channels to see what programs are on.

29

English for Tourism

John: I see. If I want to listen to some music, which channel should I change to?

F.A.: Music is offered from channels 9 to 12. There are various types of it, like pop, classical, heavy metal, rock and roll.

John: Let me try. Oh, yes. Channel 9 is offering heavy metal. It's so fantastic. Thank you! Would you please give me something cold to drink?

F.A.: Yes. We have purified water, iced tea, juice and coke. Which one do you like?

John: A glass of grape juice with ice, please.

F.A.: Here you are.

John: Sorry to have bothered you.

F.A.: My pleasure.

II. Story—retelling

Listen to the funny story and retell it using your own words. You may refer to the key words or phrases given in the box.

| rough | ocean | fasten | crash | engines |
| sharks | gel | emergency | rub | enjoy |

The Plane is Crashring into the Ocean 飞机要掉到海里啦

Flight fifty has a pretty rough time above the ocean. Suddenly a voice comes over the intercom: "Ladies and gentlemen, please fasten your seat belts and assume crash positions. We have lost our engines and we are trying to put this baby as gentle as possible down on the water."

"Oh stewardess! Are there any sharks in the ocean below?" asks a little old lady, terrified.

"Yes, I'm afraid there are some. But don't worry, we have a special gel in the bottle next to your chair designed especially for emergencies like this. Just rub the gel onto your arms and legs."

"And if I do this, the sharks won't eat me any more?" asks the lady.

"Oh, they will eat you all right, only they won't enjoy it so much."

Chapter 3　On the Flight 飞行途中

Listening for Travel 旅游听力

Useful Tips Onboard 机上有用小贴士

1. Listen to the passage twice and fill in the blanks with the information you hear (one word for one blank).

Pay close attention to the brief safety 1)_____ at the beginning of the flight and know the 2)_____ of all exits. 3)_____ is everyone's responsibility.

Be aware of which electronic devices are and are not allowed to be used during the flight. If you are 4)_____ of the rules, consult a crew member.

Follow the instructions of the crew at all times and be 5)_____ of them and the other passengers.

It is 6)_____ to behave in a manner threatening to other passengers on 7)_____ the flight. Remember, everyone has the 8)_____ to travel in a safe and secure environment.

9)_____ the crew of any disruptive behavior, follow their instructions and be polite.

Drinking juice or water during your flight instead of coffee or alcohol will help keep you hydrated.

Try doing seated leg 10)_____ throughout the flight to help prevent stiffness.

English for Tourism

2. Orally summarize the main ideas of the above passage and write them down on the following lines.

1) _____
2) _____
3) _____

Watching for Travel
旅游视频

How to Recover from Jet Lag? 怎样倒时差?

Brief information from the video:

There are a few things you could do that I want to share with you today that will help you out in your quest to avoid the doldrums of jet lag.

Drink a lot of water. It can be avoided almost entirely by drinking a lot of water. So stay hydrated during your flight. If so, you're going to be having a much better chance of retaining nutrients in your body as well as vitamins and minerals.

Set your watch the moment you get on the plane for your new destination.

Avoid alcoholic beverages and caffeine. Avoid salty snacks like nuts.

Try to sleep as much as possible on the plane.

Eat vitamins and stay healthy, and you'll overcome that jet lag within a few days.

Watch the short video twice, and complete the following requirements.

Step 1: Divide the class into groups, and ask each student to take a note of what they have watched or heard. Compare the notes with their teammates.

Chapter 3 On the Flight 飞行途中

Step 2: Make a brief summary of ways to recover from jet lag according to the video.

Summary:

1) _____

_____

2) _____

_____

3) _____

_____

4) _____

_____

5) _____

Reading for Travel 旅游阅读

Are Blind Pilots Flying? 盲人飞行员在飞吗?

1. Listen to the passage and decide whether the following statements are true or false. Write T for true and F for false.

One day at a busy airport, the passengers on a commercial airliner are seated waiting for the pilot to show up so they can get under way.

The pilot and copilot finally appear in the rear of the plane and begin walking up to the cockpit through the center aisle. Both appear to be blind; the pilot is using a white cane, bumping into passengers' right and left as he stumbles down the aisle. The copilot is using a guide dog. Both have their eyes covered with sunglasses.

At first, the passengers do not doubt thinking that it must be some sort of practical joke. After a few minutes though, the engines start revolving, and the airplane begins moving down the runway.

The passengers look at each other with some uneasiness. They start whispering among themselves and look desperately to the stewardesses for reassurance.

Yet, the plane starts accelerating rapidly, and people begin panicking. Some passengers are praying, and as the plane gets closer and closer to the end of the runway, the voices are becoming more and more hysterical.

When the plane has less than twenty feet of runway left, there is a sudden change in the pitch of the shouts as everyone screams at once. At the very last moment, the plane lifts off and is airborne.

Up in the cockpit, the copilot breathes a sigh of relief and tells the pilot: "You know, one of these days the passengers aren't going to scream, and we aren't going to know when to take off !"

1) _____ The pilot is blind, so the copilot helps him to the cockpit.

2) _____ Both the pilot and copilot wear sunglasses so that the passengers can't know whether they are really blind or not.

3) _____ At first, the passengers think it is a practical joke and do not take it seriously.

4) _____ When the plane begins moving down the runway, the passengers start to feel uneasy.

5) _____ As the plane gets closer and closer to the end of the runway, the whole cabin falls into complete quietness suddenly.

6) _____ Everyone including the pilots themselves scream at the moment the plane lifts off.

7) _____ The copilot breathes a sigh of relief because at last the plane takes off successfully.

8) _____ According to the copilot, if the passengers do not scream, the pilots won't know when to take off.

Chapter 3　On the Flight 飞行途中

Word Tips

pilot:	飞行员	cockpit:	驾驶舱
bump:	碰，撞	stumble:	蹒跚而行
revolve:	旋转	stewardess:	空中小姐
reassurance:	安心	accelerate:	加速
panic:	恐慌	hysterical:	歇斯底里的
pitch:	声调	airborne:	升空的
relief:	减轻		

2. Discuss: What kind of image a trustworthy pilot should have?

With the improvement of people's living standard, more and more people choose to travel by air. However, some people are afraid of this because of occasional happenings of air crash. So a trustworthy pilot can always play an important role to make passengers calm and relaxed.

Lead-in questions:

1) Can you imagine how the pilot and copilot in the story dress themselves?

2) If you take the plane in the story, what will you feel when you meet these two pilots?

3) What do you think a pilot should wear?

4) What qualities do you think a good and reliable pilot should have?

Group work: What kind of image a trustworthy pilot should have?

Step 1: Divide the class into groups.

Step 2: Ask students to discuss in details what kind of image a trustworthy pilot should have.

Step 3: Have some groups give their presentations in front of the class.

Singing for Travel
旅游歌曲

Take Me To Your Heart 将我带入你的心
Michael Learns To Rock

1. Singing English songs together with tourists can stimulate their interest, and liven up the atmosphere when they travel. Listen to the song casually with reference to the lyrics.

Hiding from the rain and snow

Trying to forget but I won't let go

Looking at a crowded street

Listening to my own heart beat

So many people all around the world

Tell me where do I find someone like you girl

(Chorus)Take me to your heart take me to your soul

Give me your hand before I'm old

Show me what love is - haven't got a clue

Show me that wonders can be true

They say nothing lasts forever

We're only here today

Love is now or never

Bring me far away

Take me to your heart take me to your soul

Give me your hand and hold me

Show me what love is be my guiding star

It's easy take me to your heart

Standing on a mountain high

Looking at the moon through a clear blue sky

I should go and see some friends

But they don't really comprehend

Don't need too much talking without saying anything

All I need is someone who makes me wanna sing

(Chorus)Take me to your heart take me to your soul

Give me your hand before I'm old

Show me what love is – haven't got a clue

Show me that wonders can be true

They say nothing lasts forever

We're only here today

Chapter 3 On the Flight 飞行途中

Love is now or never

Bring me far away

Take me to your heart take me to your soul

Give me your hand and hold me

Show me what love is - be my guiding star

It's easy take me to your heart

Take me to your heart take me to your soul

Give me your hand and hold me

Show me what love is - be my guiding star

It's easy take me to your heart

2. One student role plays a tour guide while others act as tourists. Sing and enjoy the English song together.

In-flight Services 机上服务

Vacation is helpful to free us from boring daily routines and various pressures of modern life. However, it also brings us other kinds of pressure. Take air travel. It is exciting and interesting to enjoy exotic scenery and culture. But taking a long-haul international flight is always hard and dull since the flight usually lasts more than 12 hours and passengers have to stay in the small cabin without much move. The journey may become even more miserable if the aircraft comes across some turbulence during the flight. Therefore, in-flight services provided by the airlines are especially important for passengers to kill time and relax themselves. Although the services are somewhat different according to the airlines, cabin classes and the distance of the journey, they can be roughly divided into the following categories.

Entertainment: In the past, entertainment just meant food and drink service. With the development of science and technology, more and more advanced equipment has been installed, which makes it possible for passengers to choose

English for Tourism

from various offerings, such as movies, TV programs, radio programs and music of different types. You can enjoy whatever you like with a complimentary headset and get relaxed.

Meal and Beverage Service: Such beverages as soft drinks, bottled purified water, milk, tea, assorted fruit juices, etc. are served free of charge while alcoholic beverages are provided free for passengers in first or business class and for purchase for those in economy class. Likewise, passengers in different cabin classes are served different meals. Usually there are several options for you. And those who have special requests can have special meals, but need to place the requests while booking the flight or going through check-in formalities.

Duty Free Shopping: An intercontinental flight offers duty free commodities, such as alcohol, fragrances, cosmetics and some other luxury goods. The price of these goods especially alcohol and tobacco is lower than that in retail shops. You can save much money, but the choice of these products is rather limited.

High-tech services: As mobile phone is not permitted to be used during the flight, you can't keep in touch with your family members and friends. This contributes to your worries. Nowadays, with the offering of satellite phone service and Internet service on international flight, this problem has been totally solved.

Read the passage aloud, and decide whether the following statements are true or false. Write T for true and F for false.

1) _____ In-flight services are somewhat different according to the airlines, cabin classes and the distance of the journey.

2) _____ Entertainment just means food and drink service.

3) _____ Alcoholic beverages are provided free of charge for all passengers during the flight.

4) _____ The price of duty free commodities offered by international flight is higher than that in retail shops.

5) _____ Now satellite phone service and Internet service have been offered on international flight.

Chapter 4

Landing at the Airport
抵达机场

Focus on Learning 学习要点

- 旅游会话　　Proper Way to Fill out the Forms　正确的填表方法
- 旅行故事　　We're Still on the Ground　我们还在地上
- 旅游听力　　Landing Announcement　飞机降落机场通知
- 旅游视频　　United Airlines Touched Down at San Francisco
　　　　　　　联合航空公司航班抵达旧金山
- 旅游阅读　　Instructions on the Declaration Form　报关表须知
- 旅游写作　　Arrival Card　入境登记卡
- 旅游歌曲　　Right Here Waiting　此情可待
- 知识扩展　　Preparations before the Plane Lands
　　　　　　　飞机降落前的准备

Useful Words and Expressions

prior to(在……之前): preceding; before

distribute(分发，分配)/dis'tribju(:)t/: to divide and give out in shares; deal out; allot

perforate(有孔的)/ 'pə:fəreit/: pierced with a hole or holes

portion(部分)/ 'pɔ:ʃən/: a part of any whole, either separated from or integrated with it

coupon(票据)/ 'ku:pɔn/: one of a set of detachable certificates that may be torn off and redeemed as needed

procedure(办事程序，步骤)/prə'si:dʒə/: an act or a manner of proceeding in any action or process; vertical, as in position or posture

standstill(停顿)/ 'stændstil/: a state of cessation of movement or action

switch off(关掉): the act or process of turning off a power supply, light source, appliance, etc.

designate(指定，标明)/ 'dezigneit/: to mark or point out; indicate; show; specify

content(内有的物品)/kən'tent/: something that is contained

fill out(填写): to write all the necessary information on an official document, form etc

capital letter(大写字母): a letter of the alphabet that usually differs from its corresponding lowercase letter in form and height, as A, B, Q and R as distinguished from a, b, q and r: used as the initial letter of a proper name, the first word of a sentence, etc.

tray table(小餐桌): a tray mounted on or in a piece of furniture, such as an airplane seatback, designed to fold or swing out of the way for storage

Chapter 4 Landing at the Airport 抵达机场

Speaking for Travel
旅游会话

I. Dialogue

Proper Way to Fill out the Forms 正确的填表方法

1. Listen to the situational dialogue carefully, and match the information in column A with that in column B.

Column A	Column B
1) form-filling requirement	A. black or blue
2) color of ink required	B. didn't write with capital letters
3) reason for asking for a new form	C. capital letters
4) set of forms required for a family	D. one set of form per family
5) person to complete the form	E. head of the household

2. Listen to the situational dialogue again, repeat it sentence by sentence, and then role play it in pairs.

Tom: Excuse me.

F.A.: Yes? How can I help you?

Tom: Could I fill out the form in blue ink?

F.A.: Yes, you can.

Tom: Good. I only have a pen with blue ink.

F.A.: Either black or blue ink is fine.

English for Tourism

Tom: All right. Thank you.

F.A.: By the way, don't forget that all the information have to be written in capital letters.

Tom: Oh, I didn't know that. I guess I need a new form. I am sorry.

F.A.: Never mind. Here you are.

Tom: By the way. Did you say all the information had to be written in capital letters?

F.A.: Yes. All the letters should be capitalized.

Tom: I am traveling with my family. Does each one of us have to fill out a custom declaration?

F.A.: No. Only one form per family is required. The head of the household should complete the form.

Tom: I see. Thank you very much.

II. Story—retelling

Listen to the funny story and retell it using your own words. You may refer to the key words or phrases given in the box.

read	air accidents	ride
worried	persuade	boarded the plane
started the engine	dangerous	take-off and landing
frightened	ants	on the ground

We're Still on the Ground 我们还在地上

Mr. Johnson had never been up in an airplane before and he had read a lot about air accidents, so one day when a friend offered to take him for a ride in his own small plane, Mr. Johnson was very worried about accepting. Finally, however, his friend persuaded him that it was very safe, and Mr. Johnson boarded the plane.

Chapter 4　Landing at the Airport 抵达机场

His friend started the engine and began to taxi onto the runway of the airport. Mr. Johnson had heard that the most dangerous part of a flight were the take-off and the landing. So he was extremely frightened and closed his eyes.

After a minute or two he opened them again, looked out of the window of the plane, and said to his friend, "Look at those people down there. They look as small as ants, don't they?"

"Those are ants," answered his friend. "We're still on the ground."

Landing Announcement 飞机降落机场通知

1. Listen to the passage twice and fill in the blanks with the information you hear (one word for one blank).

Ladies and gentlemen, welcome to Los Angeles. Please wait until the 1)_____ has come to a 2)_____ standstill before unfastening your 3)_____.

We would like to remind you that mobile phones must 4)_____ completely switched off until the seatbelt 5)_____ has been turned off.

Remember that you can only 6)_____ in designated areas once inside the terminal building.

Please take care when opening the 7)_____ lockers as the contents may have moved during the 8)_____ and might fall out and 9)_____ you or your fellow passengers.

Thank you for flying with us and we look 10)_____ to seeing you onboard with us.

43

English for Tourism

2. Orally summarize the main ideas of the above passage and write them down on the following lines.

1) _____
2) _____
3) _____

Watching for Travel
旅游视频

United Airlines Touched Down at San Francisco
联合航空公司航班抵达旧金山

Brief information from the video:

The spirit of warm San Francisco springs from the city's cultural and commercial diversity. The airport has a north and south terminal, a central terminal and an international terminal. Most united international flights arrive at concourse G of the international terminal. Because this is an international flight, all passengers must clear US immigration, claim their baggage and clear US customs in San Francisco.

Upon entering immigration, you will be directed to the appropriate lane. Every arriving passenger must complete the US custom declaration form in English in full. If the family is travelling together, the head of the household must complete the form. Please have your passport and completed travel documents ready for the immigration officer. All food and agricultural products must be declared on the US customs declaration form.

All forms must be completed in blue or black ink and write only in capital letters. It is important to accurately complete both the arrival and departure

Chapter 4 Landing at the Airport 抵达机场

records. If you are completing the green form, you must also complete the back, be sure to sign the date on the back of the green form.

If you need help completing the forms, please ask your flight attendant or United Airlines representative for assistance. Detailed instructions for completing these forms can be found in the back of your hemisphere magazine.

After clearing the immigration, proceed to the baggage claim area to reclaim your baggage. All passengers including those connecting to another flight must claim their baggage. After collecting your baggage, proceed to US customs and agriculture, and have your completed US customs form ready for the inspector.

Passengers with connecting domestic flights will recheck their baggage. Look for flight information monitors for your departure gate. United Airline's domestic flights operate from the north terminal, concourse F. It's an easy walk from the international terminal to united tickets counters and gates located in concourse F. A free shuttle bus service is also provided.

If San Francisco is your final destination, you'll exit customs to the airport arrival's hall. Currency exchange, car rental services, hotel directories and taxi, ground transportation services are available as you leave. United Airlines is a founding member of the Star Alliance, the world's leading airline alliance.

Watch the short video twice, and complete the following requirements.

Step 1: Divide the class into groups, and ask each student to take a note of what they have watched or heard. Compare the notes with their teammates.

Step 2: Make a brief summary of United Airline landing procedures to be followed according to the video.

Summary:

  1) _____
  2) _____
  3) _____
  4) _____

English for Tourism

Reading for Travel 旅游阅读

Instructions on the Declaration Form 报关表须知

1. Listen to the passage and decide whether the following statements are true or false. Write T for true and F for false. (A sample form is within the this passage)

Each individual arriving into the United States must complete the CBP Declaration Form 6059B. Explanations for information fields are explained at the end of the sample images.

1) Print your last (family) name. Print your first (given) name. Print the first letter of your middle name.

2) Print your date of birth in the appropriate day/month/year boxes.

3) Print the number of family members traveling with you (do not include yourself).

4) Print your current street address in the United States. If you are staying at a hotel, include the hotel's name and street address. Print the city and the state in the appropriate boxes.

5) Print the name of the country that issued your passport.

6) Print your passport number.

7) Print the name of the country where you currently live.

8) Print the name of the country (ies) that you visited on your trip prior to arriving to the United States.

9) If traveling by airline, print the airline's name and flight number. If traveling by vessel (ship), print the vessel's name.

Chapter 4 Landing at the Airport 抵达机场

10) Mark an X in the Yes or No box. Are you traveling on a business (work-related) trip?

11) Mark an X in the Yes or No box. Are you bringing with you:

a) fruits, plants, food, or insects?

b) meats, animals, or animal/wildlife products?

c) disease agents, cell cultures, or snails?

d) soil or have you visited a farm/ranch/pasture outside the United States?

12) Mark an X in the Yes or No box. Have you or any family members traveling with you been in close proximity of (such as touching or handling) livestock outside the US?

13) Mark an X in the Yes or No box. Are you or any family members traveling with you bringing $10 000 or more in US dollars or foreign equivalent in any form into the US?

Read definition of monetary instruments on the reverse side of the form.

Examples: *coins, cash, personal or cashier's check, traveler's checks, money orders, stocks, bonds.*

If yes, you must complete the Customs Form 4790.

14) Mark an X in the Yes or No box. Are you or any family members traveling with you bringing commercial merchandise into the US?

Examples: *all articles intended to be sold or left in the US, samples used for soliciting orders, or goods that are not considered personal effects.*

15) If you are a US resident, print the total value of all goods (including commercial merchandise) you or any family members traveling with you have purchased or acquired abroad (including gifts for someone else, but not items mailed to the US) and are bringing into the US.

Note: *US residents are normally entitled to a duty-free exemption of $800 on items accompanying them.*

If you are a visitor (non-US Resident), print the total value of all goods (including commercial merchandise) you or any family members traveling with you are bringing into the US and will remain in the US.

Note: *Visitors (non-US Residents) are normally entitled to an exemption of $100.*

English for Tourism

Declare all articles on this form. For gifts, please indicate the retail value. Use the reverse side of this form if additional space is needed to list the items you will declare.

The US Customs officer will determine duty. Duty will be assessed at the current rate on the first $1,000 above the exemption.

- Read the notice on the reverse side of the form.
- Sign the form and print the date.
- Keep the complete form with you and hand it to the CBP inspector when you approach the Customs and Border Protection area.

Controlled substances, obscene articles, and toxic substances are generally prohibited entry.

1) _____ The number of family members traveling with you should include yourself.

2) _____ If you are staying at a hotel, you don't have to write down the hotel's name and street address.

3) _____ If traveling by airline, print the airline's name and flight number.

4) _____ Visitors (non-US Residents) are normally entitled to an exemption of $100.

5) _____ Keep the complete form with you and hand it to the CBP inspector when you leave the USA.

6) _____ If traveling with other immediate family members, you just need to complete one form.

Word Tips

immediate family:	直系亲属	appropriate:	适当的
issue:	发行	vessel:	船
ranch:	农场	merchandise:	商品
entitled:	有资格的	exemption:	免税
proximity:	附近	livestock:	牲畜
equivalent:	等同物	obscene:	猥亵的
toxic:	有毒的	substance:	物质

Chapter 4 Landing at the Airport 抵达机场

2. Discuss: How to deal with the customs declaration form?

Prior to landing at any US international airport, flight attendants distribute the Customs Declaration Form to passengers. Passengers should complete these forms before landing.

Lead-in Questions:

1) Why do passengers have to fill out the customs declaration?

2) When should the form be filled?

3) What should you do if you are not sure what items should be declared?

4) What problems may you have if the form is not filled out properly?

5) When having difficulties filling out the form, what will you do?

Group Work: How to deal with the customs declaration form?

Step 1: Divide the class into groups.

Step 2: Ask students to discuss in details on the above questions and summarize the difficulties they may have when filling out the customs declaration form.

Step 3: Have some groups give their presentations in front of the class.

Arrival Card 入境登记卡

Arrival Card

Fill in an Arrival Card and present it to the immigrant officials in the airport. Make a dialogue between the tourist and immigrant officials.

English for Tourism

Family Name		Given Name				
Nationality		Date of Birth	Day	Mon	Year	☐ Male ☐ Female
Passport No.		Occupation				
Chinese Visa No.		Place of Issue				
Accompanied by						
Address in China (Hotel)		Host Organization				
Date and Flight No.		Signature				

Singing for Travel 旅游歌曲

Right Here Waiting 此情可待

Richard Marx

1. Singing English songs together with tourists can stimulate their interest, and liven up the atmosphere when they travel. Listen to the song casually with reference to the lyrics.

Oceans apart day after day

And I slowly go insane

I hear your voice on the line

But it doesn't stop the pain

If I see you next to never

How can we say forever

Chapter 4 Landing at the Airport 抵达机场

Wherever you go

Whatever you do

I will be right here waiting for you

Whatever it takes

Or how my heart breaks

I will be right here waiting for you

I took for granted' all the times

That I thought would last somehow

I hear the laughter' I taste the tears

But I can't get near you now

Oh can't you see it baby

You've got me going crazy

Wherever you go

Whatever you do

I will be right here waiting for you

Whatever it takes

Or how my heart breaks

I will be right here waiting for you

I wonder how we can survive

This romance

But in the end if I'm with you

I'll take the chance

Oh can't you see it baby

You've got me going crazy

Wherever you go

Whatever you do

I will be right here waiting for you

Whatever it takes

Or how my heart breaks

I will be right here waiting for you

Waiting for you

2. One student role plays a tour guide while others act as tourists. Sing and enjoy the English song together.

Preparations before the Plane Lands 飞机降落前的准备

Prior to landing at any US international airport, flight attendants distribute two forms to passengers (except American citizen and green card holders): a

English for Tourism

Customs Declaration Form (6059B) used to declare the value of any gifts or business items that passengers have brought with them to the US and the Arrival-Departure Record Form (I-94). Form I-94 has two specific perforated sections in it. The top portion is the arrival form that asks for information related to your arrival in the US. The bottom portion is a departure coupon and must be returned to the US officers upon exiting the US. The back side of the I-94 form is for government use only. Flight attendants also assist you with your proper completion. You will have to fill out some of your personal information like name, date of birth, passport number, your contact address in the US etc. Fill out the forms using capital letters wherever they mention TYPE or PRINT, it means you should write in capital letters. The forms should be completed before landing.

Approaching the destination, the pilot may come on the loud speaker and announce the airplane is approaching the destination and let you know what the local time is, how the weather is at the destination. Flight attendants will speak on the loud speaker, reminding you of safety procedures such as buckling up seat belts, putting seats in an upright position and turning off electronic devices.

Flight Attendants will go about the plane, checking to make sure you fasten the seat belt, seat in an upright position, and tray tables are locked up. They also make sure that all laptop computers and other electronic devices are turned off.

Read the passage aloud, and decide whether the following statements are true or false. Write T for true and F for false.

1) _____ Prior to landing at any US international airport, flight attendants distribute one form to passengers.

2) _____ Flight attendants distribute forms to passengers except American citizen and green card holders.

3) _____ A departure coupon must be returned to the US officers upon exiting the US.

4) _____ You have to fill in both sides of the form.

5) _____ All laptop computers and other electronic devices should be turned off when approaching the destination.

Chapter 5

Tourism Transportation
旅游交通

Focus on Learning 学习要点

- 旅游会话　　Travel by Taxi 搭乘出租车
- 旅行故事　　The Train Has Broken Down 火车开不动了
- 旅游听力　　Travel by Train in the USA 美国火车旅游
- 旅游视频　　Cabs in New York City 纽约出租车
- 旅游阅读　　Interesting Things about Transport 交通工具趣闻
- 旅游歌曲　　Scarborough Fair 斯卡堡集市
- 知识扩展　　Railway in the United States 美国的铁路交通

Useful Words and Expressions

reluctant(不情愿的，勉强的)/riˈlʌktənt/: unwilling; disinclined

express(迅速的)/iksˈpres/: direct or fast

reserve(预订或保留)/riˈzəːv/: to keep back or save for future use

compartment(卧车包房)/kəmˈpɑːtmənt/: a private bedroom with toilet facilities

variation(变化)/ˌvɛəriˈeiʃən/: the act, process, or accident of varying in condition, character, or degree

roving(徘徊的，移动的)/ˈrəuviŋ/: roaming or wandering

jaunt(短途游览)/dʒɔːnt/: a short journey, esp. one taken for pleasure

rugged(高低不平的)/ˈrʌgid/: having a roughly broken, rocky, hilly, or jagged surface

landscape(风景)/ˈlændskeip/: a section or expanse of rural scenery, usually extensive, that can be seen from a single viewpoint

spectacular(壮观的)/spekˈtækjulə/: of or like a spectacle; marked by or given to an impressive, large-scale display

accessible(可接近的)/əkˈsesəbl/: easy to approach, reach, enter, speak with, or use

prairie(大草原)/ˈprɛəri/: an extensive area of flat or rolling, predominantly treeless grassland, esp. the large tract or plain of central North America

prospector(探矿者)/prɔˈspektə(r)/: one who explores an area for mineral deposits or oil

Chapter 5 Tourism Transportation 旅游交通

I. Dialogue

Travel by Taxi 搭乘出租车

1. Listen to the situational dialogue carefully, and match the information in column A with that in column B.

Column A	Column B
1) destination	A. Peter's
2) traveler's requirement for the restaurant	B. the subway
3) driver's recommendation for the restaurant	C. good restaurants downtown that offer meals at a reasonable price
4) driver's preference for the means of transportation	D. the Broadway
5) reason not to take a bus	E. have to transfer a couple of times

2. Listen to the situational dialogue again, repeat it sentence by sentence, and then role play it in pairs.

Lisa: Hey, taxi! Thanks for pulling over.

Driver: Where to?

Lisa: I am going to the Broadway.

Driver: This is your first time to the city, right?

Lisa: Yeah. How did you know?

English for Tourism

Driver: Well, I can tell tourists from far away because they walk down the street looking straight up at the skyscrapers.

Lisa: Is it that obvious?

Driver: Well. It is quite easy to tell.

Lisa: Oh, before I forget, can you recommend any good restaurants downtown that offer meals at a reasonable price?

Driver: Well, the Mexican restaurant, Peter's, is fantastic. It's not as inexpensive as other places I know, but the decor is very authentic, and the portions are larger than most places I've been to.

Lisa: Sounds great! How can I get there from the Broadway?

Driver: Well, you can catch the subway. There are buses running that way, but you would have to transfer a couple of times. And there are taxis too, but it is not easy to hail one at rush hours.

Lisa: OK. Thanks.

II. Story-retelling

Listen to the funny story and retell it using your own words. You may refer to the key words or phrases given in the box.

| engine | break down | half power | standstill |
| inform | announcement | fly | |

The Train Has Broken Down 火车开不动了

A large two engined train was crossing America. After it had gone some distance, one of the engines broke down. "No problem", the engineer thought, and carried on at half power.

Farther on down the line, the other engine broke down neither, and the train came to a standstill.

The engineer decided he should inform the passengers about why the train had stopped, and made the following announcement:

Chapter 5　Tourism Transportation 旅游交通

"Ladies and gentlemen, I have some good news and some bad news. The bad news is that both engines have failed, and we will be stuck here for some time. The good news is that you decided to take the train and not fly."

Listening for Travel 旅游听力

Travel by Train in the USA 美国火车旅游

1. Listen to the passage twice and fill in the blanks with the information you hear (one word for one blank).

Many wonderful long-distance trains 1)＿＿＿＿ in the United States, often travelling through wild, spectacular 2)＿＿＿＿ not easily accessible any other way. The following are among the most highly recommended 3)＿＿＿＿.

The Coast Starlight is one of Amtrak's most scenic trips for travel by train and a particular favorite with 4)＿＿＿＿ people. A party 5)＿＿＿＿ frequently develops, starting in the lounge car and 6)＿＿＿＿ throughout the train as it journeys between Seattle and Los Angeles. You see snow-covered 7)＿＿＿＿, forest valleys and long stretches of the Pacific shoreline.

The California Zephyr is one of the world's greatest journeys, taking two days and nights to travel by train between Chicago and San Francisco, 8)＿＿＿＿ farmland, prairie, 9)＿＿＿＿, rivers and the Rocky Mountains. Western pioneers came this way, as did gold prospectors, the Pony Express and the first 10)＿＿＿＿ line. The Zephyr follows America's earliest transcontinental rail route for much of its 2 420-mile journey.

English for Tourism

2. Orally summarize the main ideas of the above passage and write them down on the following lines.

1) _____

2) _____

3) _____

Watching for Travel 旅游视频

Cabs in New York City 纽约出租车

Basic information from the video:

Know where you're going. Before you hail a cab, get a rough idea of how far you're going and how much it should cost. If you're not sure, ask a New Yorker.

Step off the curb and face the oncoming traffic. Just don't step so far off the curb that you're standing in a lane of traffic.

Hail a cab by raising your arm when you spot one with its middle roof light on.

Avoid busy areas. Don't try to hail a cab just slightly in front of someone else with their arm out—it's rude. If you're in an area where lots of people are trying to get cabs, walk a few blocks to a less competitive location. Try hailing an off-duty cab by indicating with your fingers that you're only going a short distance, he might just take you.

Enter and exit on sidewalk. Play it safe by always getting in—and out—of the cab on the same side as the sidewalk.

Chapter 5 Tourism Transportation 旅游交通

Know your rights. You have the right to tell the driver which route to take, you can ask him to slow down, and you are in control of the heat, AC, and radio. If the driver says he doesn't go outside Manhattan, politely contradict him and make a note of his medallion number, so you can report him if need be.

Buckle up. Better safe than sorry.

Watch the meter. When you hop in the cab, the fare starts at $2.50. The meter will increase 40 cents every fifth of a mile or, if you're standing still or crawling along slowly, once every minute. No extra charge for luggage. On weekdays from 4 p.m. to 8 p.m., there's an extra $1 surcharge. And every night after 8 p.m., there is a night surcharge of 50 cents.

Know airport fares. La Guardia is a regular metered fare, but you're also responsible for any tolls along the way. Note that New York City cabs can drop you at Newark airport, but because it's out of state, they're not legally allowed to pick up fares.

Pay the fare. and unless you had the worst ride of your life, add a nice tip. 10 to 20 percent tip is customary.

Get a receipt. It has the taxi's medallion number on it, which will come in handy if you accidentally leave something in the cab.

Watch the short video twice, and complete the following requirements.

Step 1: Divide the class into groups, and ask each student to take a note of what they have watched or heard. Compare the notes with their teammates.

Step 2: Make a brief summary of ways to survive the ride in New York according to the video.

Summary:

1) _____
2) _____
3) _____
4) _____
5) _____

English for Tourism

Reading for Travel 旅游阅读

Interesting Things about Transport 交通工具趣闻

1. Survey: Take this fun quiz to find out some facts about transport.

1) A tunnel goes under water or through mountains. Where is the longest railway tunnel in the world? (　　)

    A. between Switzerland and France.

    B. between the UK and France

    C. in Japan

2) The first airplane flight was made in 1903. How long was it? (　　)

    A. 12 seconds.

    B. 2 minutes and 12 seconds.

    C. 12 minutes.

3) The first bike with two wheels was invented in Germany in 1816. What was strange about the bike? (　　)

    A. You could only go in a straight line!

    B. You had to pedal the bike with your hands.

    C. It didn't have any pedals——you had to move it with your feet.

4) In 1999 Brian Jones and Bertrand Piccard flew around the world in a hot air balloon. How long did it take? (　　)

    A. 4 days, 7 hours and 22 minutes.

    B. 14 days, 19 hours and 51 minutes.

    C. 24 days, 21 hours and 8 minutes.

5) In 1912 the Titanic was the biggest passenger ship in the world. It sank on its first trip. Why? (　　)

    A. There was a big storm.

    B. It hit a big piece of ice.

Chapter 5　Tourism Transportation 旅游交通

　　C. There was a big fire.

　　6) The first car was made in 1908. It was very expensive. Which was the first cheap car that people could afford? (　　)

　　　　A. the Model T from Ford

　　　　B. the Rolls Royce

　　　　C. the Karl-Benz

　　7) Where is the highest train station in the world? (　　)

　　　　A. Bolivia　　　　B. Japan　　　　C. India

　　8) In February 2001 Ellen MacArthur was the fastest woman to travel alone around the world (　　).

　　　　A. in a sailing boat　　B. on a tricycle　　C. in a helicopter

　　9) In London people travel on an underground railway. What is it called? (　　)

　　　　A. the metro　　　　B. the tube　　　　C. the line

　　10) A limousine is a very long car. How long is the longest limousine in the world? (　　)

　　　　A. 15 meters　　　　B. 22.5 meters　　　　C. 30.5 meters

Word Tip

| tunnel: | 隧道 | pedal: | 踩踏板 |
| helicopter: | 直升机 | limousine: | 豪华轿车 |

---

　　2. Discuss: What's your preference, public transportation or private car?

　　There are so many means of transportation, such as buses, taxis, subways and airplanes. Buses are cheap but a little slow. Airplanes are fast but a little dear. It costs much money to get to the destination. Work with you partner and discuss.

　　Lead-in questions:

　　1) What forms of public transportation are there in your country?

　　2) How do you travel to school or work, by bus or by bike? Do you walk or

English for Tourism

go by other means of transportation?

3) What are the advantages and disadvantages of using public transportation instead of driving your own car to get to school or work?

4) Do universities or companies provide their students or employees a pass for free?

5) Which do you prefer, public transportation or private cars? State your reasons.

Group Work: What's your preference, public transportation or private car?

Step 1: Divide the class into groups.

Step 2: Ask students to discuss in details the above questions and summarize.

Step 3: Have some groups give their presentations in front of the class.

Singing for Travel 旅游歌曲

Scarborough Fair 斯卡堡集市

Sarah Brightman

1. Singing English songs together with tourists can stimulate their interest, and liven up the atmosphere when they travel. Listen to the song casually with reference to the lyrics.

Are you going to Scarborough Fair	Tell her to make me a cambric shirt
Parsley, sage, rosemary and thyme	
Remember me to one who lives there	Parsley, sage, rosemary and thyme
She once was a true love of mine	Without no seams nor needle work

Chapter 5　Tourism Transportation 旅游交通

Then she will be a true love of mine

Tell her to find me an acre of land

Parsley, sage, rosemary and thyme

Between the salt water and the sea strand

Then she will be a true love of mine

Tell her to reap it with a sickle of leather

Parsley, sage, rosemary and thyme

And gather it all in a bunch of heather

Then she will be a true love of mine

Are you going to Scarborough Fair

Parsley, sage, rosemary and thyme

Remember me to one who lives there

She once was a true love of mine

2. One student role plays a tour guide while others act as tourists. Sing and enjoy the English song together.

Additional Know-how 知识扩展

Railway in the United States 美国的铁路交通

If you're tired of flying or if you are reluctant to drive for days on unfamiliar roads, a train trip may be a good choice. Train travel makes transportation an enjoyable and valuable part of your journey as opposed to a necessary displeasure; you can see miles of countryside as you gently speed towards your destination.

Long-distance travel by train is not as common in the USA as it many other parts of the world. Most train travel is in the northeast part of the country, linking Boston, New York, Philadelphia, Baltimore and Washington, D.C.. Special express trains travel between New York and Washington, D.C.. All seats on these trains are reserved in both coach (2nd class) and club car (1st class). Long-distance trains also serve major cities such as Atlanta, Miami,

… New Orleans, Chicago, Los Angeles, San Francisco and Seattle. Sleeping compartments are available on most long-distance trains and must be reserved in advance.

Most trains are operated by AMTRAK, the national railroad corporation. The number for buying ticket is 800-USA-RAIL. AMTRAK currently offers three variations on its USA Rail Pass, which is good for travel across the USA. The USA Rail Pass is not valid on select trains. The pass is available to both US and international citizens. Amtrak also offers a California Rail Pass, which is good for seven days of economy-class travel in California over a 21-day period. You can get a sleeper car and make the train your roving hotel as you take a cross-country jaunt through some of the most beautiful, rugged landscapes in the world. Amtrak offers a number of scenic routes that will help you to slow down and get a good look at the world outside your window.

Read the passage aloud, and decide whether the following statements are true or false. Write T for true and F for false.

1) _____ Long-distance travel by train is common in the USA.
2) _____ Sleeping compartments are available on most long-distance trains and must be reserved in advance.
3) _____ AMTRAK is a private railroad corporation.
4) _____ You can buy USA Rail Pass if you want to travel across the United States.
5) _____ The USA Rail pass is only available to USA citizens.

Chapter 6

Hotel Check-in
入住酒店

> **Focus on Learning 学习要点**

- 旅游会话　　　Changing Reservation 改订房间
- 旅行故事　　　Don't Treat Us like We're a Couple of Fools
　　　　　　　别把我们当成一对傻瓜
- 旅游听力　　　Tips for Hotel Reservation 酒店预订技巧
- 旅游视频　　　Hotel and Front Desk Clerk 酒店和度假村前台人员
- 旅游阅读　　　Documents for Hotel Check-in 入住酒店证件
- 旅游写作　　　Laundry Registration 衣物清洗表
- 旅游歌曲　　　Sunny Came Home 阳光走进家门
- 知识扩展　　　Front Desk/Reservation Desk 前台

Useful Words and Expressions

beverage(酒水)/ˈbevəridʒ/: (formal) any sort of drink except water, e.g. milk, tea, wine, beer

cashier(出纳员/收银员)/kəˈʃiə/: a person who receives and pays out money in a bank, store, hotel, restaurant, etc.

accumulate(累积)/əˈkjuːmjuleit/: make or become greater in number or quantity

transaction(交易)/trænˈzækʃən/: a piece of business that is done between people, especial an act of buying or selling

register(登记)/ˈredʒistə/: make a written and formal record of, in a list

crucial(关系重大的)/ˈkruːʃiəl/: decisive; critical

entail(使必要)/inˈteil/: make necessary; impose (expense, etc. on sb.)

recession(不景气)/riˈseʃən/: slackening of business and industrial activity

check out(离店结账): to vacate and pay for one's quarters at a hotel

double room(双人房间): a type of hotel accommodation with two beds, or sometimes a double bed, for occupancy by two person

single room(单人房间): a type of hotel accommodation with one bed for occupation by one person

limousine(豪华轿车)/ˈlimu(ː)ziːn/: any large, luxurious automobile, esp. one driven by a chauffeur

Chapter 6　Hotel Check-in 入住酒店

Speaking for Travel 旅游会话

I. Dialogue

Changing Reservation 改订房间

1. Listen to the situational dialogue carefully, and match the information in column A with that in column B.

Column A	Column B
1) reason for calling	A. Sam Brown
2) caller's name	B. Nov. 1 to Nov. 3
3) original date of reservation	C. to make some reservation changes
4) new date of reservation	D. limousine
5) extra service	E. from Nov. 1 to Nov. 4

2. Listen to the situational dialogue again, repeat it sentence by sentence, and then role play it in pairs.

Clerk: Good morning, room reservation. How can I help you?

Sam: Yes, my name is Sam. I made a reservation, but I'd like to make some changes.

Clerk: Under whose name was the reservation made?

Sam: Sam Brown.

Clerk: What was the date of the reservation?

English for Tourism

Sam: From Nov. 1 to Nov. 3. But the check-out date should be on Nov. 4. And I need a double room instead of a single room.

Clerk: A double room from Nov. 1 to Nov. 4. Is that correct?

Sam: Yes.

Clerk: Do you need a limousine service?

Sam: That's just what I want. How much does it charge?

Clerk: $40. We have a counter at the airport where our representatives will lead you to the car.

Sam: It sounds nice. I'll take that.

Clerk: Thank you, sir. We look forward to serving you.

II. Story-retelling

Listen to the funny story and retell it using your own words. You may refer to the key words or phrases given in the box.

| Backwoods | celebrate | anniversary | plush hotel | settle for |
| Fools | because | complain | elevator | |

Don't Treat Us like We're a Couple of Fools
别把我们当成一对傻瓜

A couple had lived together in the backwoods for over fifty years. To celebrate their fiftieth anniversary, the husband took his wife to a large city, and they checked into a plush hotel.

The wife said to the bellman, "We refuse to settle for such a small room. No windows, no bed, and no air conditioning."

"But, madam!", replied the bellman.

"Don't 'But madam' me," she continued. "You can't treat us like we're a couple of fools just because we don't travel much, and we've never been to the big city, and never spent the night at a hotel. I'm going to complain to the manager."

"Madam," the bellman said, "this isn't your room; this is the elevator!"

Chapter 6　Hotel Check-in 入住酒店

Listening for Travel 旅游听力

Tips for Hotel Reservation 酒店预订技巧

1. Listen to the passage twice and fill in the blanks with the information you hear (one word for one blank).

You can almost guarantee a great price on any hotel package or airfare by making your 1)_____ very early, at least a month or so before your trip. In this way, you'll be locked into a low price. Additionally, while there may be some 2)_____, look for off-peak deals at most major hotels. This may 3)_____ a mid-week stay. If you're looking for a weekend getaway, consider booking your hotel on a Thursday with a Monday 4)_____. Because hotels are feeling the pinch during this recession just like the rest of us, call them directly and find out what types of packages they're currently offering. They may be willing to present you with a 5)_____ that precisely fits your time frame and 6)_____.

If you really want to save on hotel 7)_____, choose bed-and-breakfast 8)_____, smaller hotels or inns. Remember, they're 9)_____ for your business as well. For example, a two-bedroom suite at an East Hampton Inn during off-peak seasons can be gotten for less than $100 per night. 10)_____ rates typically run close to $300 a night for the very same room. Quite a difference, wouldn't you say?

English for Tourism

2. Orally summarize the main ideas of the above passage and write them down on the following lines.

1) _____
2) _____
3) _____

Watching for Travel
旅游视频

Hotel and Front Desk Clerk 酒店和度假村前台人员

Brief information from the video:

The front desk clerk is usually the first person a guest encounters when checking into a hotel or motel. In addition to performing the specific duties, he has the responsibility of making a great first impression. It is important for him to be able to quickly and efficiently follow the steps to get the guest check in.

It's essential for him to be knowledgeable about the checking-out times, hotel services and local attractions. What's more, he should have qualities such as: personal warmth, friendliness, and good interpersonal skills.

He should make the tired and stressed customers feel truly welcomed and comfortable when they reach the hotels so that they'll make a point of staying at the hotel.

The front desk is an excellent place to start if you are interested in career of hotel management since you can learn about many different aspects involving in running a hotel efficiently and places you on the front line of customer relations.

Chapter 6 Hotel Check-in 入住酒店

Watch the short video twice, and complete the following requirements.

Step 1: Divide the class into groups, and ask each student to take a note of what they have watched or heard. Compare the notes with their teammates.

Step 2: Make a brief summary of front desk clerk's major qualifications according to the video.

Summary:

1) _____
_____

2) _____
_____

3) _____
_____

4) _____
_____

5) _____
_____

Documents for Hotel Check-in 入住酒店证件

1. Listen to the passage and decide whether the following statements are true or false. Write T for true and F for false.

While checking into a hotel, you'll need to prove that you are the person who made the reservation either in person, over the phone, or through travel agency. You are required to provide your identification documents such as a driver's license, state ID card or passport. There are two reasons for front desk clerk to require your identification. The first reason is to protect customers from fraudulent credit card use and theft. Requiring identification upon check-in is a way that hotels can ensure that a hotel room was not booked with a stolen credit card. The second reason is to protect your safety. Requiring an ID for check-in is a way to make sure that only registered, paid guests like you are admitted to hotel rooms, and prevents strangers or criminals from comprising the personal safety of those staying in the hotel.

Moreover, you may also need to present a reservation confirmation which can guarantee you a room under no circumstances. If you book a hotel room online, you will usually be e-mailed a confirmation statement with a special confirmation number that guarantees your reservation. If you book over the phone, through a travel agent or in person, you'll often be given a printout with your confirmation number on it. For example, if the hotel has made a mistake and shows no record of your reservation, but you have a printed confirmation from them, they will have to accommodate you even if they are fully booked up. However, not all hotels provide confirmation letters. Some hotels will simply give you a confirmation number over the phone when you make your reservation.

Other documentations that you should have on hand when checking into hotels include the credit card you used to make your reservation, or your checkbook, as well as any letters or licenses pertaining to special medical or personal needs. These include doctor's letters regarding medical conditions or dietary restrictions, and permits for seeing-eye dogs that allow guests to bring their animal guides into hotels with no pet policies.

1) _____ When checking into a hotel, you are required to provide your identification documents.

Chapter 6 Hotel Check-in 入住酒店

2) _____ One of the reasons for asking for ID is to ensure that guests are using their own credit cards.

3) _____ All hotels provide confirmation letters that guarantee guests' reservations.

4) _____ You can only get a confirmation statement through internet.

5) _____ The hotel staff will have to accommodate you if they don't have your booking record, but you have a confirmation statement from them.

6) _____ What you need for hotel checking-in are: identification documents, reservation confirmation, credit card or check book, and letter for special medical or personal care.

Word Tips

fraudulent:	欺诈的	criminal:	罪犯
comprise:	构成	guarantee:	保证
accommodate:	提供住宿	pertain to:	关于
dietary:	饮食的		

2. Discuss: What documents do you need for hotel check-in?

Generally speaking, hotel check-in process is simple, quick and hassle-free. Hotel front desk clerks are friendly and ready to assist guests with any concerns they might have. Yet a smooth and satisfactory check-in also needs your cooperation. Work with your partner and discuss the following questions.

Lead-in Questions:

1) Have you or any of your friends got any experience in hotel check-in?

2) What are the reasons for presenting your identification?

3) Do you think your reservation confirmation number is important, and why?

English for Tourism

4) What happen if you have the confirmation, yet the hotel does not have your booking record?

5) If you will pay your bill in cash or check, will you provide your credit card information when asked, and why?

Group Work: What documents do you need for hotel check-in?

Step 1: Divide the class into groups.

Step 2: Ask students to discuss in details on the above questions and summarize the required documents you need to present while checking in. Give sufficient reasons.

Step 3: Have some groups give their presentations in front of the class.

Laundry Registration 衣物清洗表

Fill in the Laundry Registration and present it to the maid. Make a situational dialogue accordingly.

Beijing Holiday Inn   No.

Name:	PLEASE TICK ONE
Signature:	☐ REGULAR SERVICE-GARMENTS RECEIVED BEFORE 10:00 A.M. RETURNED THE SAMEDAY
Date Room No.	☐ EXPERSS SERVICE-GARMENTS RECEVIE BEFORE 2:00 P.M RETURNED THE SAMEDAY

SPECIAL SERVICE: ☐REPAIRING
☐BUTTONING   ☐STAIN-REMOVING

Chapter 6　Hotel Check-in 入住酒店

续表

GUEST COUNT	HOTEL COUNT	LADIES	UNIT PRICE	AMOUNT	GUEST COUNT	HOTEL COUNT	GENTLEMEN	UNIT PRICE	AMOUNT
		BLOUSE	¥4.00				BATHROBE	¥5.00	
		BRASSIERE	¥2.00				DRESS SHIRT	¥1.00	
		DRESS	¥8.00				HANDKERCHIEF	¥4.00	
		HANDKERCHIEF	¥1.00				PYJAMA(SET)	¥4.00	
		EVENING DRESS	¥10.00				NORMAL SHIRT	¥4.00	
		UNDERPANTS	¥2.00				SHORTS	¥1.00	
		PYJAMA(SET)	¥4.00				SOCK	¥5.00	
		SHORTS	¥4.00				SWEATER	¥3.00	
		SKIRT	¥6.00				SWIMSHORT	¥6.00	
		SKIR(PLEATED)	¥15.00				TROUSERS	¥3.00	
		SLACKS	¥6.00				T-SHIRT	¥2.00	
		SOCKS(PAIRE)	¥1.00				UNDERPANTS	¥2.00	
		STOCKINGS	¥1.00				VEST	¥4.00	
		SUIT(2PCES)	¥15.00				SPORTS SHIRT	¥10.00	
		SWEATER	¥9.00				WAFUKU	¥9.00	
		T-SHIRT	¥3.00						
		UNDERSHIRT	2.00						

1. GUEST IS REQUIRED TO COMPLETE THE LIST, OTHERWISE HOTEL COUNT MUST BE ACCEPTED AS CORRECT.
2. THE HOTEL IS NOT RESPONSIBLE FOR VALUABLES IN POCKETS.
3. IN CASE OF LOSS OR DAMMAGE, THE HOTEL WILL BE LIABLE TO NO MORE THAN TEN TIMES THE REGULAR PROCESSING CHARGE OF THE ITEM.
4. ALL CLAIMS MUST BE MADE WITHIN 24 HOURS AFTER DELIVERY AND MUST BE ACCOMPANED BY THE ORIGINAL LIST.

SPECIAL INSTRUCTIONS
BASIC CHARGE　　　　　¥
50% EXTRA CHARGE FOR EXPRESS ¥
10% SERVICE CHARGE　　¥
GRAND TOTAL　　　　　¥
BILLED BY:

English for Tourism

Singing for Travel
旅游歌曲

Sunny Came Home 阳光走进家门
Shawn Colvin

1. Singing English songs together with tourists can stimulate their interest, and liven up the atmosphere when they travel. Listen to the song casually with reference to the lyrics.

Sunny came home to her favorite room

Sunny sat down in the kitchen

She opened a book and a box of tools

Sunny came home with a mission

She says days go by I'm hypnotized

I'm walking on a wire

I close my eyes and fly out of my mind

into the fire

Sunny came home with a list of names

She didn't believe in transcendence

It's time for a few small repairs she said

Sunny came home with a vengeance

She says days go by I don't know why

I'm walking on a wire

I close my eyes and fly out of my mind

Into the fire

Get the kids and bring a sweater

Dry is good and wind is better

Count the years, you always knew it

Strike a match, go on and do it

Days go by I'm hypnotized

I'm walking on a wire

I close my eyes and fly out of my mind

Into the fire

light the sky and hold on tight

The world is burning down

She's out there on her own and she's alright

Sunny came home

Sunny came home ...

2. One student role plays a tour guide while others act as tourists. Sing and enjoy the English song together.

76

Chapter 6   Hotel Check-in 入住酒店

Additional Know-how
知识扩展

Front Desk/Reservation Desk 前台

Front Desk is also called Reception Desk. It is the nerve center of a hotel. Its major function is to act as the public face of a hotel, primarily by greeting hotel guests and checking in guests. It also provides assistance and services to guests during their stay, completes their accommodation, food and beverage, account and receives payment from guests.

Functions of a Front Desk can be grouped into five general categories:

- reception
- bell service
- mail and information
- concierge
- cashiers and night auditors

There will be two major departments involved in the above list. Employees staffing the first four categories belong to room department. Employees working in the fifth category belong to financial department, where guest charges are accumulated and posted to bills, and all cash transactions are accomplished.

Staff of Front Desk welcome you, carry your luggage, help you register, give you the room keys and mail, answer questions about the activities in the hotel and surrounding area, handle complaints from dissatisfied guests, and finally check you out. They have the responsibility to make you a great first impression on the hotel and make you feel you are very welcomed. Their positive impression made on you will be crucial to a hotel's success. It is of importance for them to be able to work quickly and efficiently to follow all steps to get you check into the hotel. Moreover, they should be knowledgeable about check-out time, hotel service, local attraction and more.

Read the passage aloud, and decide whether the following statements are true or false. Write T for true and F for false.

1) _____ Front desk is different from reservation desk.

2) _____ The major function of a front desk is to act as a public face of the hotel.

3) _____ Functions of a front desk can be grouped into five categories; and front desk involves three departments.

4) _____ Front desks have the responsibility to make you a great first impression on the hotel and make you feel you are very welcomed.

5) _____ Front desk should be knowledgeable about check-out time only.

Chapter 7

Hotel Check-out 退房结账

Focus on Learning 学习要点

- 旅游会话　A Late Check-out 延时退房
- 旅行故事　The Hotel Bill 饭店账单
- 旅游听力　How to Save Money on Hotel Bills? 怎样节省酒店开支？
- 旅游视频　A Checklist for Check-out 退房结账清单
- 旅游阅读　Avoid Extra Hidden Fees 避免额外的隐性费用
- 旅游歌曲　I still believe 我仍然相信
- 知识扩展　ABC for Hotel Check-out 退房结账常识

Useful Words and Expressions

attendant(服务员)/əˈtendənt/: a person who attends guests, as to perform a service

inform(通知)/inˈfɔ:m/: to give or impart knowledge of a fact or circumstance to

in advance(预先): ahead in time; beforehand

evaluation(评估)/i,væljuˈeiʃən/: an act or instance of evaluating or appraising

brochure(小册子)/brəuˈʃjuə/: a pamphlet or leaflet

bellboy(侍者)/ˈbelbɔɪ/: a bellhop, a person whose job is to carry people's cases to their rooms in a hotel

corporate(团体的)/ˈkɔ:pərit/: pertaining to a united group, as of persons

voucher(凭证)/ˈvautʃə(r)/: a document, receipt, stamp, or the like, that gives evidence of an expenditure

acknowledgement(承认)/əkˈnɔlidʒmənt/: recognition of the existence or truth of something

arrange(安排)/əˈreindʒ/: to prepare or plan

regulation(规定)/regjuˈleiʃən/: a law, rule, or other orders prescribed by authority, esp. to regulate conduct

reception desk(前台): a counter, as at a hotel, in which guests are registered, also called front desk.

Chapter 7 Hotel Check-out 退房结账

Speaking for Travel
旅游会话

I. Dialogue

A Late Check-out 延时退房

1. Listen to the situational dialogue carefully, and match the information in column A with that in column B.

Column A	Column B
1) guest's name	A. 1:00 p.m.
2. room number	B. it's too early to go to the airport
3. reason for requiring a late check-out	C. Jill Smith
4. due time for cleaning up the room	D. use the business center, free of charge
5. solution to the problem	E. room 812

2. Listen to the situational dialogue again, repeat it sentence by sentence, and then role play it in pairs.

Clerk:　　Good morning, Ms.. Can I help you?

Jill:　　Good morning. I'm Jill Smith in room 812. I'm leaving today. But can I check out a little bit late?

Clerk:　　Why?

Jill:　　You see, my plane takes off at 6:30 this afternoon. But I don't want to go to the airport so early.

Clerk: It's really a problem. But your room has been reserved, and we have to clean it up before 1:00 p.m..

Jill: Then can I leave at 2 o'clock?

Clerk: Well, you can't, since the guests will check-in at 2:00 p.m.. I can arrange you to another room, but according to hotel's regulations, during the high season, you should pay half of the daily room rate if you leave before 6 p.m..

Jill: I don't think it's reasonable. Can I speak to your manager?

Clerk: OK. I'll call our manager.

Manager: Ms., what can I do for you?

Jill: I'm asking for a late check-out since my plane won't take off until 6:30 p.m..

Manager: (...) Your room has been reserved for a newly married couple, and they'll check in at 2:00p.m.. How about going to our business center, free of charge?

Jill: Thank you. That helps me a lot.

Manager: My pleasure. Hope to serve you better next time.

II. Story-retelling

Listen to the funny story and retell it using your own words. You may refer to the key words or phrases given in the box.

travel	tired	continue	hotel	four hours
check out	$350	high	facilities	complain

The Hotel Bill 饭店账单

A husband and wife are traveling by car from Key West to Boston. After almost 24 hours on the road, they're too tired to continue, and they decide to stop for a rest. They stop at a nice hotel and take a room, but they only plan to sleep for four hours and then get back on the road. When they check out four hours

Chapter 7　Hotel Check-out 退房结账

later, the desk clerk hands them a bill for $350.

The man explodes and demands to know why the charge is so high. He tells the clerk although it's a nice hotel, the rooms certainly aren't worth $350. When the clerk tells him $350 is the standard rate, the man insists on speaking to the Manager. The Manager appears, listens to the man, and then explains that the hotel has many facilities such as an Olympic-sized pool and a huge conference center that the man and wife could have made use of.

"But we didn't use them", the man complains.

"Well, we have them, and you could have", the Manager replies.

Eventually the man gives up and agrees to pay. He writes a check and gives it to the Manager. The Manager is surprised when he looks at the check.

"But sir," he says, "this check is only made out for $100."

"That's right," says the man, "I charged you $250 for using my car—a Mercedes-Bens."

"But I didn't!" exclaims the Manager.

"Well," the man replies, "it was here, and you could have."

Listening for Travel 旅游听力

How to Save Money on Hotel Bills? 怎样节省酒店开支？

1. Listen to the passage twice and fill in the blanks with the information you hear (one word for one blank).

When traveling, the most expensive things are 1)_____ the flight and hotel bills. The following is some steps to save money on hotel 2)_____.

Step 1: To save money on hotel bills, you should ask for the hotels corporate rate when making a reservation. Corporate rates are often much

3)_____ than the normal room prices and most hotels have these corporate 4)_____.

Step 2: Many hotels require that you stay at least 8 nights per year to 5)_____ for the corporate rate. To get around this, you can write a letter to the hotel using your company's 6)_____. Most hotels will give the corporate rate to anyone who does this.

Step 3: If you are using a travel agent to help you book the room, make sure you get a confirmation number which 7)_____ your room. A travel agent will give you a voucher but this has no 8)_____ acknowledgement from the hotel.

Step 4: To save money on hotel bills, shop around for the best pricing 9)_____. Speaking with many hotels about their corporate rates is the best way to book a room at a very 10)_____ rate.

2. Orally summarize the main ideas of the above passage and write them down on the following lines.

1) _____
2) _____
3) _____

A Checklist for Check-out 退房结账清单

Brief information from the video:

But take a look at this hotel checkout checklist, and you won't be smacking yourself in the forehead when you get back. Check it out.

Chapter 7　Hotel Check-out 退房结账

Take your time packing before you check out. Allowing yourself a few extra minutes to calmly get everything back into your suitcase will reduce your chances of carelessly forgetting anything. If you're pressed for time, you can always call the front desk and request a late checkout, which will often buy you another hour.

Do a complete sweep of the room. Once everything obvious is in your bags, be sure to check all the nooks and crannies. As you're about to leave the room, do one final pass over the entire area——and be sure to check under the covers, too.

Leave a tip. Leave cash in the amount of three to five bucks per night at a fancy hotel, and one or two at a less fancy joint, and be sure to leave it in a properly marked envelope.

When checking out, be sure to review your entire bill. Check that all of the charges are exact, and make sure you have a paper statement or receipt to walk away with. Remember that now is the time to dispute anything funky—the second you walk out the door, it gets a little bit tougher.

Watch the short video twice, and complete the following requirements.

Step 1: Divide the class into groups, and ask each student to take a note of what they have watched or heard. Compare the notes with their teammates.

Step 2: Make a brief summary of ways to make sure that nothing will be left behind when you check out at a hotel according to the video.

Summary:

1) _____
2) _____
3) _____
4) _____
5) _____

English for Tourism

Reading for Travel
旅游阅读

Avoid Extra Hidden Fees 避免额外的隐性费用

1. Listen to the passage and decide whether the following statements are true or false. Write T for true and F for false.

Checking out of some hotel rooms can give you a serious case of shock. With taxes, room service, phone charges and other "hidden" fees, that $199 deal you booked online can turn into a $379 bill. Keep these tips in mind on your next stay to keep your hotel bill within your budget.

Telephone Charges:

Check how much the phone charges are at each hotel you stay in. Many hotels charge as much as $1.50 (or more) for local phone calls. And long distance rates can be unconscionably high. Before you make a call, check the rates. They should be posted somewhere in the room. If you don't see them, call the front desk and ask. Better yet, use your cell phone for all calls, even local.

Room Service:

Room service is expensive. An "American Breakfast" (two eggs, bacon, toast, coffee and juice) can cost upwards of $30. Avoid ordering it if possible. Walk down to the hotel restaurant to order, or better yet, walk down the street.

When you do order room service, pay close attention to the fees tacked on to the bill. Many hotels charge a "delivery charge" of several dollars added to the already steep prices. Plus, most room service bills automatically add a 15-18

Chapter 7 Hotel Check-out 退房结账

percent gratuity. Overlooking this can cause you to over-tip, so beware.

Internet Access:

Many hotels are adding high-speed Internet access to their amenities. This is a great service if you are doing a lot of work online while on the road. Be aware that there is usually a charge for this service (generally $10 per day). If you have time, it's cheaper to stop in at a nearby coffee shop that offers free Wi-Fi. Also, many hotels that charge for Internet access in the rooms, offer it free of charge in the lobby, so ask.

Mini Bar:

If you have late-night food cravings, plan ahead and pack accordingly. Otherwise, that 3 a.m. mini bar may cost you five bucks. It tempts you by stocking tasty snacks, alcohol and other luxuries right in your room for convenience, but you are definitely paying for it.

Bellman:

In some hotels, the bellman situation is getting out of control. Sometimes, there are several bellmen: one to help your luggage out of the cab, one to bring it to the bell stand, and one to take it to your room. That's a lot of tipping. Save yourself the aggravation and buy a "Bellman Buster"—a suitcase on wheels—and wheel it to your room yourself.

Resort Fees:

Resort fees are daily charges hotels add to your bill for things you might expect to be free, like access to the fitness center or swimming pool and daily newspaper delivery. The fees can range from ten dollars a day upwards of thirty or forty dollars, impacting your bill quite a bit. You should be informed of resort fees when you check in. If you don't plan to use the facilities included in the resort fee, the best time to protest the fee is when you are checking in. Ask to speak to a manager and make your case.

If the resort fee includes tips to bell staff, you should understand that no

English for Tourism

additional tips are necessary. Pay attention when you are checking in to what you are signing; better yet, ask about a resort fee at the time you book your room at any resort.

1) _____ Telephone charges at many hotels are unreasonably high.

2) _____ When you order room service, pay close attention to the fees tacked on the bill.

3) _____ Many hotels charge for Internet access both in the rooms and in the lobby.

4) _____ According to the writer, bellman situation at some hotels is getting out of control.

5) _____ Resort fees are daily charges hotels add to your bill for things you might expect to be free.

6) _____ If you don't plan to use the facilities included in the resort fee, the best time to protest the fee is when you are checking out.

Word Tips

deal:	交易	budget:	预算
unconscionably:	过度地	tack:	把……固定住
steep:	过高的	gratuity:	小费
beware:	当心	access:	进入
amenity:	消遣设施	craving:	渴望
accordingly:	相应地	buck:	美元
stock:	提供	luxury:	奢侈品
convenience:	便利	definitely:	肯定地
aggravation:	恼怒	resort:	游览胜地
facility:	设施	protest:	反对
additional:	额外的		

Chapter 7　Hotel Check-out 退房结账

2. Discuss: If you are charged unreasonably, what will you do?

Nowadays, traveling has been widely accepted as a way of life. And it is natural for people to expect a palatable travel experience. However, such an experience may be spoiled by unreasonable charges happening here and there. So how to deal with unreasonable charges is important to have a happy and unforgettable travel experience.

Lead-in Questions:

1) Do you think it is necessary to check the bill carefully whenever you check out from the hotel?

2) Do you have the experience of being unreasonably charged?

3) Will you talk in a good manner or in a temper?

4) If you cannot reach an agreement with the hotel staff, what will you do, keeping on arguing or settling it with wisdom? How?

5) What will you do if you still have dispute even if you talk to a manager?

Group Work: If you are charged unreasonably, what will you do?

Step 1: Divide the class into groups.

Step 2: Ask students to discuss in details what they will do if they are charged unreasonably.

Step 3: Have some groups give their presentations in front of the class.

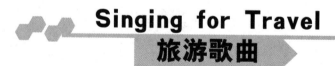

I Still Believe 我仍然相信

Mariah Carey

1. Singing English songs together with tourists can stimulate their

English for Tourism

interest, and liven up the atmosphere when they travel. Listen to the song casually with reference to the lyrics.

You look in my eyes and I get emotional inside

I know it's crazy, but you still can touch my heart

And after all this time you think that I wouldn't feel the same

But time melts into nothing and nothing has changed

I still believe, someday you and me

Will find ourselves in love again

I had a dream, someday you and me

Will find ourselves in love again

Each day of my life

I'm filled with all the joy I could find

You know that

I am not the desperate type

If there's one spark of hope left in my grasp

I'll hold it with both hands

It's worth the risk of burning

To have a second chance

No, no, no, no, no, I need you, baby

I still believe that we can be together, no...

If we believe that true love never has to end

Then we must know that we will love again

I still believe, someday you and me

Will find ourselves

In love again (Oh, baby, yeah)

I had a dream, you and me

Will find ourselves, in love again

I still believe (Ooh, baby, I do)

Someday you and me (Just give me one more try)

In love again

I had a dream (I miss your love)

Someday you and me

Will find ourselves in love again

I still believe (Yeah, I still believe)

Someday you and me (Baby, yeah)

2. One student role plays a tour guide while others act as tourists. Sing and enjoy the English song together.

Chapter 7 Hotel Check-out 退房结账

Additional Know-how 知识扩展

ABC for Hotel Check-out 退房结账常识

When you check in at a hotel, usually the attendant at the reception desk will inform you of the check-out time so that when you need to check out you can do it before that time and avoid being charged extra fee. Generally the check-out time in most hotels is 12 o'clock. And you need to pay half of the daily room rate if you check out between 12 p.m. and 18 p.m. or pay a full day's room rate if you check out after 18 p.m.. However, if you have to require a late check-out, you should contact the reception desk before 10 a.m. on the day of departure. The hotel will usually try to satisfy you for free or with a charge.

English for Tourism

In order to avoid spending too much time going through check-out formalities, especially during the high season when there is a crowd of guests checking in or checking out, you'd better call the reception desk at least thirty minutes earlier to inform them so that they can get your bill prepared in advance.

Before you check out, a room attendant may go up and check up the room thoroughly to make sure that everything is all right. In addition, he/she will also check whether you have consumed or damaged anything. If so, he/she will make an evaluation and require you to pay for these items when you check out. The price of every item in the room has been printed in the room service brochure. So when you consume something or damage something, you'd better browse through the brochure and find the price of these items so that you can check whether there is a mistake in the bill or not.

Usually a bellboy will be arranged to help you with your luggage when you leave the room. At the reception desk, you need to return the room card and confirm the bill. If there is no mistake, you can sign it and make the payment.

Read the passage aloud, and decide whether the following statements are true or false. Write T for true and F for false.

1) _____ Generally the check-out time in most hotels is 12 o'clock.

2) _____ You need to pay half of the daily room rate if you check out after 18 p.m..

3) _____ If you have to require a late check-out, you should contact the reception desk before 8 a.m. on the day of departure.

4) _____ When you want to check out, you'd better call the reception desk at least thirty minutes earlier to inform them.

5) _____ When you check out, you'll be charged for the items you have consumed or damaged in the room.

Chapter 8

Theme Parks 主题公园

➡ Focus on Learning 学习要点

- 旅游会话　　Disneyland Theme Park 迪斯尼主题公园
- 旅行故事　　Roller Coaster 过山车
- 旅游听力　　Tips for Saving Tickets to Theme Parks
　　　　　　　主题公园门票省钱窍门
- 旅游视频　　A Travel to Universal Studio of Hollywood
　　　　　　　好莱坞环球电影制片公司之旅
- 旅游阅读　　A Brief Introduction of the Disneyland
　　　　　　　迪斯尼乐园简介
- 旅游写作　　Cruising on the Huangpu River 巡游黄浦江
- 旅游歌曲　　Hotel California 加州旅馆
- 知识扩展　　A Money-and-Time Effective Way to Visit Theme Parks
　　　　　　　省钱省时玩转主题公园

Useful Words and Expressions

roller coaster(过山车): a small gravity railroad, esp. in an amusement park, having a train with open cars that moves along a high, sharply winding trestle built with steep inclines that produce sudden, speedy plunges for thrill-seeking passengers

route(路线)/ruːt/: a particular way of direction between places

priority(优先)/praiˈɔriti/: something must be dealt with as soon as possible and before other less important things

convenient(方便的)/kənˈviːnjənt/: suitable for your needs and causing the least difficulty

wane(衰退)/wein/: weaken in strength or influence

stamp(压印)/stæmp/: to print (a design, lettering, a date, etc.) on paper, cloth or other surface

invalid(无效的)/inˈvælid/: void or lack of legal force

parade(游行)/pəˈreid/: a large public procession, often of a festival nature

preview(预告)/ˈpriːvjuː/: an opportunity to see something before it is shown to the public

distinct(明显不同的)/disˈtiŋkt/: clearly separate and different from something else

royalty(王室)/ˈrɔiəlti/: the people who belong to the family of a king and queen

distinguish(使显著)/disˈtiŋgwiʃ/: to provide an unusual quality which makes something noticeably different from or better than others of the same type

savor(品味)/ˈseivə/: to enjoy(food or an experience)slowly, in order to appreciate it as much as possible

tribute(称颂)/ˈtribjuːt/: something that shows respect and admiration for someone, esp. on a formal occasion

Chapter 8 Theme Parks 主题公园

Speaking for Travel
旅游会话

I. Dialogue

Disneyland Theme Park 迪斯尼主题公园

1. Listen to the situational dialogue carefully, and match the information in column A with that in column B.

Column A	Column B
1) park location	A. expensive ticket prices
2) first trouble	B. Hong Kong
3) second trouble	C. invalid tickets
4) result	D. student discount
5) discount enjoyed	E. caught the man and got the money back

2. Listen to the situational dialogue again, repeat it sentence by sentence, and then role play it in pairs.

David: How's your trip to Disneyland in Hong Kong?

Amy: Oh, very special. It's like on an emotional roller coaster.

David: What happened?

Amy: At first my boyfriend and I were excited to go because we thought we'd get in with no problem. Then when we got there, we found out the tickets were selling for a lot more than we'd planned, which almost made us leave.

English for Tourism

David: You didn't book online? It can save you a lot.

Amy: No, we were foolish enough to forget that. But we finally managed to get a deal with someone to get two cheap tickets.

David: Good for you!

Amy: But the tickets turned out invalid. We hadn't noticed that. It was hot and we were eager to get in.

David: Oh, I'm sorry.

Amy: Don't be. The drama was that just when we were giving up all the hope, we saw the ticket man. We called the police and got our money back.

David: Lucky you!

Amy: Then we were told we could enjoy a discount with our student cards. That's how we finally got into the park.

David: Great! Did you like it?

Amy: Loved it, especially the cartoon character parade! It made me relive my childhood.

II. Story-retelling

Listen to the funny story and retell it using your own words. You may refer to the key words or phrases given in the box.

ride	the roller coaster	hill	decide
get off	explain	impossible	shriek
scream	realize	in the name of	

Roller Coaster 过山车

When my granddaughter Betty is about 6 years old and goes to ride the roller coaster with her father one day. At the top of the hill she decides that she wants to get off. She turns to her dad and tells him to stop the thing and get her off. Her dad explains it is impossible. Betty shrieks all the way down the first hill

Chapter 8　Theme Parks 主题公园

while her dad explains once again that he cannot do it. Betty screams down the second hill. Going up the third hill, and the last one, Betty realizes that her father cannot stop the coaster. She shouts at the top of her lungs, "In the name of Jesus Christ get thee behind me roller coaster!"

Tips for Saving Tickets to Theme Parks
主题公园门票省钱窍门

1. Listen to the passage twice and fill in the blanks with the information you hear (one word for one blank).

Visiting a theme park for the day with a family of four can add up. But there are ways to cut costs.

Look for Internet specials and 1)_____ in newspapers, on products, and at gas stations and fast food chains. Your employer may also have a 2)_____ discount rate for local parks. AAA offers many theme park and attraction discounts and 3)_____ when tickets are purchased in advance through AAA. You might even call the park to ask about 4)_____ if you don't see one on the website. Most attractions will help you find the best deals available if you just ask.

The day and time you visit affects prices too. Some parks 5)_____ less if you arrive in the late afternoon, and often they are open in summer and on weekends until 10 p.m. or later — perfect for 6)_____. Nighttime visits also may enjoy mean fewer crowds, cooler temperatures and no 7)_____. If you do pay full price late in the day, some attractions will give you the next

English for Tourism

day free. Many attractions offer discounted tickets if you plan a 8)_____ visit.

If you live near a small 9)_____ park or old-fashioned seaside park, these can be considerably cheaper than big theme parks, with much shorter lines. Some parks have discounts for 10)_____.

2. Orally summarize the main ideas of the above passage and write them down on the following lines.

1) _____
2) _____
3) _____

Watching for Travel
旅游视频

A Travel to Universal Studio of Hollywood
好莱坞环球电影制片公司之旅

Brief information from the video:

My favorite part of Universal Studios of Hollywood is the studio tour.

It's my chance to show you real Hollywood movie making on the world famous backlot.

There is devastation created for the site of World War II and the giant life-like character from King Kong.

You can experience the explosive hard driving action of The Fast and the Furious and visit the sites of award-winning TV shows.

Chapter 8 Theme Parks 主题公园

Watch the short video twice, and complete the following requirements.

Step 1: Divide the class into groups, and ask each student to take a note of what they have watched or heard. Compare the notes with their teammates.

Step 2: Make a brief summary of ways to travel around Universal Studio of Hollywood according to the video.

Summary:

1) _____
2) _____
3) _____
4) _____
5) _____

A Brief Introduction of the Disneyland 迪斯尼乐园简介

1. Listen to the passage and decide whether the following statements are true or false. Write T for true and F for false.

Disneyland is an American theme Park in Anaheim, California, owned and operated by the Walt Disney Parks and Resorts division of The Walt Disney Company. It was dedicated with a press preview on July 17, 1955, and opened to the general public the following day. Disneyland holds the distinction of being the only theme park to be designed, built, opened, and operated by Walt Disney.

Currently the park has been visited by more than 515 million guests since it opened, including presidents, royalty and other heads of state. In 1998, the theme

English for Tourism

park was re-branded "Disneyland Park" to distinguish it from the larger Disneyland Resort complex. In 2007, over 14 800 000 people visited the park making it the second most visited park in the world, behind the Magic Kingdom at Walt Disney World.

In 1955, on its open ceremony, Walt Disney said to the public, "To all who come to this happy place—welcome. Disneyland is your land. Here age relives fond memories of the past and here youth may savor the challenge and promise of the future. Disneyland is dedicated to the ideals, the dreams, and the hard facts that have created America ... with the hope that it will be a source of joy and inspiration to all the world." From then on, the dedication to all Disney magic kingdom-style parks begins with the phrase "To all who come to this happy place—welcome ..." with the exception of Magic Kingdom Park in Florida. The dedication there begins "Walt Disney World is a tribute to the philosophy and life of Walter Elias Disney ..."

1) _____ Disneyland was opened to the public on July 17,1955.

2) _____ Besides Disneyland, Walt Disney had also designed and operated other theme parks.

3) _____ A lot of celebrities have visited Disneyland since its opening.

4) _____ Disneyland was re-branded to make it sound more fantastic.

5) _____ The most visited park in the world also belongs to the Disney Company.

6) _____ The dedication to all the Disney theme parks around the world begins with what Walt said on the opening day.

Word Tips
resort:胜地   press:新闻   preview:预告
distinction:殊荣   currently:目前   royalty:皇室
savor:品尝   dedicate:奉献   philosophy:哲学

Chapter 8　Theme Parks 主题公园

2. Discuss: How much do you know about Disneyland?

Disneyland is said to be children's heaven while adults regard it as a getaway from the routine of the daily life. Work with you partner and discuss.

Lead-in Questions:

1) Have you even been to a Disneyland Park? If not, are you interested in going? Why or why not?

2) Do you know after whom Disneyland was named?

3) What do you believe makes Disneyland so popular?

4) How much do you know about the story of Walt Disney? What can you learn from him?

5) How much do you know about the two Disney Park in Los Angeles?

Group Work: How much do you know about Disneyland?

Step 1: Divide the class into groups.

Step 2: Ask students to discuss in details about the above questions and summarize.

Step 3: Have some groups give their presentations in front of the class.

Writing for Travel 旅游写作

Commentary 导游词

Read the commentary and write a commentary of a tourist site that you know and make a presentation in your class. Pay attention to your body language.

Cruising on the Huangpu River 巡游黄浦江

Ladies and gentlemen, now we are at the Bund (外滩) of the Huangpu River. I sincerely hope every one of you will have a good time here. Today, we'll have a cruise on the Huangpu River and see the past and the present of Shanghai. Cruising on the river can also give you a better chance to see the different views of both sides of the river-Pudong(浦东) and Puxi(浦西).

Attention please! On your left-hand is the wide Zhongshan Road(中山路) where the marvelous buildings with European style tower majestically. You can watch "the World Architecture Show"("万国建筑博览"). On your right-hand are the glistening Huangpu River and Lujiazui Finance Trade Area(陆家嘴金融贸易区) in Pudong. You may watch the Oriental Pearl TV Tower(东方明珠电视塔), a landmark of the New Shanghai.

Look across the river! What a magnificent building complex with the western style! In front of us is the Dongfeng Hotel(东风饭店). This is a building in classical British style. In the past it was the British General Assembly(英国总领馆). The six-storey building is topped with two pavilions in the north and south. The interior of the building is decorated luxuriously. There used to be a 110. 7 inch-long bar counter on the first floor, the longest one in Asia at that time. At present, KFC is located there.

Look at the building with a circular roof in Greek style! It is the famous building of former Hong Kong & Shanghai Bank(汇丰银行). The building with five storeys was built in 1923. Plus its dome top, it altogether has 7 storeys. It had reception rooms of the American, British, French, Russian and Japanese styles. The British was proud of it and regarded it as the best building in the area from the Suez Canal to the Far East. Not long ago it was the office building of Shanghai Municipality.

Ladies and gentlemen, did you see the building next to the former Shanghai & Hong Kong Bank? On the top of it, there is a big clock. It is the Shanghai Customs Building(上海海关大楼) built in 1927. The clock strikes every 15 minutes, and gives out a short piece of music. You can check you time accordingly because it gives you the standard Beijing time. The former Shanghai & Hong Kong Bank and the Customs Building were designed by a famous British designer. People in Shanghai called them "Sister Buildings". At present,

Chapter 8　Theme Parks 主题公园

they remain an important landmark of Shanghai.

Please look at the other side of the river! A tower is piercing straight to the clouds and sky. It is the Oriental Pearl TV Tower, the new landmark of Shanghai. The 468-meter Orient Pearl TV Tower is the tallest building in Asia and the third tallest TV tower in the world. Our travel boat is leaving the Oriental Pearl TV Tower. And more scenic sites are waiting for us ahead! If you missed the chance to take pictures, don't worry! And you can take photos when we come back. Tonight we'll have our dinner in the rotating restaurant of the Tower. You can have a bird's view of the night of Shanghai on the sightseeing floor.

Thank you for having joined us.

Singing for Travel 旅游歌曲

Hotel California 加州旅馆
The Eagles

1. Singing English songs together with tourists can stimulate their interest, and liven up the atmosphere when they travel. Listen to the song casually with reference to the lyrics.

On a dark desert highway	I had to stop for the night
Cool wind in my hair	There she stood in the doorway
Warm smell of colitas	I heard the mission bell
Rising up through the air	
Up ahead in the distance	And I was thinking to myself
I saw a shimmering light	This could be Heaven or this could be Hell
My head grew heavy, and my sight grew dim	Then she lit up a candle

English for Tourism

And she showed me the way

There were voices down the corridor

I thought I heard them say

Welcome to the Hotel California

Such a lovely place

Such a lovely place (background)

Such a lovely face

Plenty of room at the Hotel California

Any time of year

Any time of year (background)

You can find it here

You can find it here

Her mind is Tiffany twisted

She got the Mercedes bends

She got a lot of pretty, pretty boys

That she calls friends

How they dance in the courtyard

Sweet summer sweat

Some dance to remember

Some dance to forget

So I called up the Captain

Please bring me my wine

He said

We haven't had that spirit here since 1969

And still those voices are calling from far away

Wake you up in the middle of the night

Just to hear them say

Welcome to the Hotel California

Such a lovely Place

Such a lovely Place (background)

Such a lovely face

They livin' it up at the Hotel California

What a nice surprise

What a nice surprise (background)

Bring your alibies

Mirrors on the ceiling

The pink champaign on ice

And she said

We are all just prisoners here

Of our own device

And in the master's chambers

They gathered for the feast

They stab it with their steely knives

But they just can't kill the beast

Last thing I remember

I was running for the door

I had to find the passage back

To the place I was before

"Relax", said the nightman

We are programmed to receive

You can check out any time you like

But you can never leave

2. One student role plays a tour guide while others act as tourists. Sing and enjoy the English song together.

Chapter 8　Theme Parks 主题公园

Additional Know-how
知识扩展

A Money-and-Time Effective Way to Visit Theme Parks
省钱省时玩转主题公园

For most theme park goers, the most horrible part may not be the roller coaster but the seemingly endless waiting in front of every big attraction and pricey food and drinks. How can you get the most from your theme park visit in a money-and-time effective way?

Here is some advice that might help you. First, plan your visit ahead. Print out a direction map for the theme park. If it is a busy route, you can find another route to go to, so you can get there earlier. And unless the park is small, you shouldn't expect to see or do everything in one day, so set your priorities to save on unnecessary decision-making time. Second, buy tickets in advance, you can save up to 25% off ticket prices if you buy ahead of time and you do not have to wait on the long line before the entrance. The internet is always a good choice to find the best price. Third, arrive early. By arriving 15 minutes early, you can spare yourself nearly one hour waiting time for the most popular attractions. Think about it before you decide to drive all your way up there. While it is fast and easy, it also means about half an hour waiting time for the parking space. Thus if there is convenient public transportation, use it. Besides, for the driver, the route drive there is great, but after one exciting day at the theme park, the driving may be painful on your way home. Forth, remember that theme parks are usually spread out all over the place, and they are huge.

Therefore, use a monorail or train if they are available to get around in the park. They are very helpful, especially on hot days. Fifth, bring bottled water. The prices of food and drinks in the parks are very costly, but sadly, most corporate parks do not allow outside food and drink, unless it's water. Always check its policy before visiting. In that case, you can save both your money and time. It is always surprising so many people are willing to line up 20 minutes just to get a hot dog in the parks.

Generally, theme parks are most crowded in the middle of the day. This is a good time to rest for a few hours—regaining your strength for another visit on the park later in the day. Leave mid-day to freshen up. When the energy of other guests wanes late day, go back into the park. This time, visit the attractions closer to the entrance first where it is probably less crowded now. But be sure to get your hand stamped or get some other proof of admission that will allow you to be readmitted to the park at no charge. While taking your mid-day break from the park, remember to eat outside. It is less expensive and the service is usually faster and better.

Read the passage aloud, and decide whether the following statements are true or false. Write T for true and F for false.

1) _____ Getting the park map before visit can save you time.
2) _____ Public transportation is a better choice than private cars when visiting the park.
3) _____ Usually, you are not allowed to take any food or drink into those corporate theme parks.
4) _____ During the day you cannot leave the park then return there free of charge.
5) _____ The food outside the park is less expensive but the service is rather poor.

Chapter 9

Get-together
聚会派对

➡ Focus on Learning 学习要点

- 旅游会话　　A Cocktail Party 鸡尾酒会
- 旅行故事　　Free Advice at Social Affairs 社交聚会上的免费建议
- 旅游听力　　A Bonfire Party 篝火晚会
- 旅游视频　　How to Deal with Unexpected Guests?
　　　　　　如何应对不速之客？
- 旅游阅读　　How to Throw a Surprise Party?
　　　　　　如何举办惊喜聚会？
- 旅游歌曲　　Only Time 唯有时光
- 知识扩展　　A Successful Party 成功的派对

Useful Words and Expressions

spice(情趣)/spaɪs/: interest or excitement, esp. as added to something else

company(陪伴)/ˈkʌmpəni/: the presence of another person; companionship

informative(增进知识的)/inˈfɔːmətiv/: providing useful facts or ideas

inspiring(激励人心的)/inˈspaɪərɪŋ/: that gives one the urge or ability to do great things; providing inspiration

elaborate(精心制作的)/ɪˈlæbərət/: worked out with great care and nicety of detail; executed with great minuteness

lack of(缺乏): the state of not having enough of something

consequence(结果)/ˈkɔnsikwəns/: the effect, result, or outcome of something occurring earlier

ruin(毁掉)/ruin/: to destroy or spoil

ensure(确保)/inˈʃuə/: to make sure or certain

atmosphere(气氛)/ˈætməsfiə/: the general character or feeling of a place

decorate(装饰)/ˈdekəreit/: to furnish or adorn with something ornamental or becoming; embellish

venue(举办场所)/ˈvenjuː/: the place where something is arranged to happen

priority(优先考虑的事)/praiˈɔriti/: something that needs attention, consideration, service, etc., before others

torch(火把)/tɔːtʃ/: a mass of burning material tied to a stick and carried by hand to give light

Chapter 9　Get-together 聚会派对

I. Dialogue

A Cocktail Party 鸡尾酒会

1. Listen to the situational dialogue carefully, and match the information in column A with that in column B.

Column A	Column B
1) guest's name	A. monogrammed wine stopper
2) type of the party	B. champagne on the rocks
3) present brought to John	C. Jennifer
4) other drinks prepared	D. cocktail party
5) drink required	E. gin, rum and champagne

2. Listen to the situational dialogue again, repeat it sentence by sentence, and then role play it in pairs.

John:　　Hi. Jennifer. Come in, please.

Jennifer:　Hi. John. Thank you for inviting me to the party. This is for you.

John:　　That's very nice of you. Wow, a monogrammed wine stopper. I like it very much. Thank you.

Jennifer:　I'm glad you like it.

John:　　You're really nice to me. So what would you like to drink?

English for Tourism

Jennifer: What cocktails do you have?

John: Well, Cosmopolitan, Dirty Martini, Chocolate Martini and Apple Martini.

Jennifer: These are the most popular drinks for cocktail parties these days. But today I'd like to have something else. Are there any other drinks?

John: Gin, rum and champagne.

Jennifer: A glass of champagne on the rocks, please.

John: Here you are. You see, there are so many friends. Go around and make yourself at home.

Jennifer: I will. Thank you.

II. Story-retelling

Listen to the funny story and retell it using your own words. You may refer to the key words or phrases given in the box.

doctor	lawyer	cocktail party	approach
medical advice	handle	turn to	situation
acceptable	send	certainly	

Free Advice at Social Affairs 社交聚会上的免费建议

A doctor and a lawyer were attending a cocktail party when the doctor was approached by a man who asked advice on how to handle his ulcer. The doctor mumbled some medical advice, then turned to the lawyer and remarked, "I never know how to handle the situation when I'm asked for medical advice during a social function. Is it acceptable to send a bill for such advice?" The lawyer replied that it was certainly acceptable to do so.

The next day, the doctor sent the ulcer-stricken man a bill. The lawyer also sent one to the doctor.

Chapter 9   Get-together 聚会派对

Listening for Travel 旅游听力

A Bonfire Party 篝火晚会

1. Listen to the passage twice and fill in the blanks with the information you hear (one word for one blank).

A bonfire party is usually not a party you send invitations out for. They usually 1)_____ spontaneously on summer nights. There are a great way to get out in the fresh air and enjoy the 2)_____ of nature, as well as a few dozens of your 3)_____ friends.

Bonfire parties must be held outdoors. The best location is one that is obscure and somewhat 4)_____. There are a couple of different outdoor areas that would probably be better choices than others. A 5)_____ is the best location to have a bonfire, especially one by a small pond. The 6)_____ best is in a sandy pit.

After carefully choosing a 7)_____ to have your bonfire, you must make a few preparations. These include some amount of 8)_____ such as firewood, something to start the fire with, roasting sticks, tables, chairs, coolers, tools for 9)_____ the fire and various kinds of food. Besides, entertainments and games are also important to make your bonfire 10)_____ and enjoyable.

2. Orally summarize the main ideas of the above passage and write them down on the following lines.

1) _____
2) _____
3) _____

English for Tourism

Watching for Travel 旅游视频

How to Deal with Unexpected Guests? 如何应对不速之客？

Brief information from the video:

Be polite. As the perfect host, your first priority is to accommodate the surprise arrival. Put them at their ease, welcome them into your home and offer them a drink.

Squeeze them in. While they are busy talking to the other guests, disappear into the dinning room and squeeze another place onto the table set up.

Split the portions. If dinner is a serve yourself affair, then the extra guest is easy to accommodate—simply adjust the portions accordingly. However, if you have prepared six portions of chicken—not seven—then you have no alternative but to split delightful niece Tara's portion with her surprise partner.

Speak to offender afterwards. Either in private or after the event you are perfectly entitled to make your delightful niece realize that her actions were completely unacceptable.

Watch the short video twice, and complete the following requirements.

Step 1: Divide the class into groups, and ask each student to take a note of what they have watched or heard. Compare the notes with their teammates.

Step 2: Make a brief summary of ways to deal with unexpected guests according to the video.

Summary:

1) _____

2) _____

3) _____

Chapter 9　Get-together 聚会派对

Reading for Travel 旅游阅读

How to Throw a Surprise Party? 如何举办惊喜聚会？

1. Listen to the passage and decide whether the following statements are true or false. Write T for true and F for false.

Planning any event can be pretty stressful, so throwing a surprise party can be a little trickier, with the added fact that you and all the guests have to keep the party secret from the person whom the party is for. Here are some tips to help make organizing the party easier.

Guest List:

Writing a guest list should be one of the first things you decide to do. As you are throwing a surprise party, inviting people that the surprise guest has not seen for some time is often done. If you have not got the contact details for these people, asking someone who lives with the surprise guest is an option, they may be able to get hold of their address book or even contact some people themselves.

If you know that someone will not be able to keep the surprise party a secret, then it is best to treat them as you would the surprise guest and not let them know what you are planning, just telling them the date they need to keep free. Just one person leaking the event will ruin the surprise, so be careful who you tell.

Date:

Deciding on when the party is to be thrown is very important as you will need to ensure that the surprise guest and everyone else are able to attend on this date. You will need to come up with a cover up story on why you want the surprise guest to book time in their diary. Weekends or bank holidays are usually the best days to hold an event as more people will be able to attend.

Venue:

Once a date has been decided, a venue will need to be booked. You will need to choose a suitable venue that will accommodate your needs and budget. Make sure the venue is accessible for everyone who is attending, for example is it easy enough to find, is there enough car parking spaces etc.

There are so many venues that can cater for surprise parties. Here are the most popular choices:

House party—If you are planning a party on a budget or want a more personal touch, then this is a good option. You can tell the surprise guest that they are invited to yours for a meal.

Function Room—Most bars, hotels, clubs etc. have a function room which they hire out. Prices tend to vary and can be based on per hour, set room, per person etc. There are many function rooms that are free to hire. Do a search on the internet, look in your local phone book, and ask around.

Restaurant—If you do not want to plan a party but still want a surprise celebration, then booking space in a restaurant can be ideal. Many restaurants have separate rooms for large bookings.

Final Arrangements:

Tell all the guests to arrive at the party earlier than the surprise guest, half an hour is usually a good time, this way people who never turn up on time will have half an hour leeway before the surprise guest arrives.

It is advised to get someone to arrive with the surprise guest so they do not have an idea what is going on and if anything goes wrong at the other end, for example, you are running late, the food has not arrived etc. and you need the guest to arrive later than planned you can contact the other person and let them know.

1) _____ According to the writer, to throw a surprise party is more difficult because you and all the guests should keep it a secret from the person whom the party is for.

2) _____ If you know that someone will not be able to keep the surprise party a secret, it is best not to invite them.

3) _____ As you are throwing a surprise party, you'd better invite those that the surprise guest has not seen for some time.

4) _____ To make sure that the surprise guest and everyone else can be able to attend the party, you'd better choose weekends and bank holidays to hold it.

5) _____ If you do not want to plan a party but still want a surprise

Chapter 9 Get-together 聚会派对

celebration, a function room is the best choice.

6) _____ When you choose a venue for the party, make sure that it is accessible to every guest.

7) _____ It is better to tell other guests to arrive at the party thirty minutes earlier than the surprise guest.

8) _____ It is not necessary to get someone to arrive with the surprise guest if you have everything ready.

Word Tips

throw:	举行(聚会)	fabulous:	极好的
tricky:	棘手的	leak:	走漏
ruin:	毁掉	venue:	举办地点
budget:	预算	leeway:	灵活性
accessible:	易接近的	function room:	功能厅
cater for:	满足……的要求		

2. Discuss: If you are to throw a surprise party, what will you do?

Parties provide occasions for people to gather with friends and enjoy themselves. Good parties are always wonderful and inspiring experiences. However, to hold such a party is not easy. We have to work hard for a well-prepared party.

Lead-in Questions:

1) How can you make sure that all the guests would keep the party as a secret from the surprise guest?

2) When do you think is an appropriate time to hold the party?

3) What is the appropriate time for other guests to arrive at the party?

4) Do you think it is necessary to have someone arrive with the surprise guest?

5) How to deal with these guests who are unable to keep the surprise party as a secret?

Group Work: If you are to throw a surprise party, what will you do?

Step 1: Divide the class into groups.

115

English for Tourism

Step 2: Ask students to discuss in details on the above questions and summarize what they will do to throw a surprise party.

Step 3: Have some groups give their presentations in front of the class.

Singing for Travel 旅游歌曲

Only Time 唯有时光

Enya

1. Singing English songs together with tourists can stimulate their interest, and liven up the atmosphere when they travel. Listen to the song casually with reference to the lyrics.

Who can say where the road goes	In your heart
Where the day flows	And who can say when the day sleeps
Only time...	If the night keeps all your heart
And who can say if your love grows	Night keeps all your heart...
As your heart chose	Who can say if your love grows
Only time...	As your heart chose
Who can say why your heart sighs	Only time...
As your love flies	And who can say where the road goes
Only time...	Where the day flows
And who can say why your heart cries	Only time...
When your love dies	Who knows
Only time...	Only time...
Who can say when the roads meet	Who knows
That love might be	Only time...

2. One student role plays a tour guide while others act as tourists. Sing and enjoy the English song together.

Chapter 9 Get-together 聚会派对

Additional Know-how 知识扩展

A Successful Party 成功的派对

Parties are the spice of life. They are the time to gather with friends, laugh, talk, play games and enjoy one another's company. However, it is not easy to hold an informative, inspiring and successful party. You must be very careful to organize everything well and try to make it go smoothly. To achieve it, there are some steps you need to be aware of and follow.

First, set a theme for your party. Usually you need to have a reason to hold a party and gather your friends together. The reason is not necessarily an elaborate one. You may celebrate the returning of a loved one, the birthday of a family member or the graduation of your child, etc.

Second, plan it carefully. When and where the party will be held? What type of party will you hold? And do you need a co-host or some helpers? How many guests will you invite? You need to take all of these into consideration and make a careful preparation. Lack of planning may lead to some unexpected consequences and ruin the party.

Third, make a good guest list. When you make the guest list, you'd better think it over and avoid inviting those who do not get along with others and who have ever caused troubles in the past. Make sure that all of the guests are friendly so as to ensure a good atmosphere at the party.

Fourth, send out invitations. Usually you need to send out invitations four or six weeks in advance so that the guests may have time to consider and rearrange their schedules. If it is an informal party, you can just call the guests or invite them face-to-face. But keep in mind all of these should be done ahead of time.

Fifth, decorate the venue properly. Once you decide the venue of the party, spend some time thinking about how to decorate it to match the atmosphere. While doing this, you need to put top priority to safety and security. For example,

English for Tourism

if you want to use large flaming torches, you'd better think whether they can be safely put away from the guests. Otherwise, you may choose other replacements such as candles.

Sixth, create proper atmosphere. The aim of a party is to entertain guests and make them have a good time. So preparing some funny events and games are very important for the success of the party. But you should make sure that the events and games are completely different from what you have offered in the past.

Seventh, plan your food list and shop several days ahead of time. Once you set the theme of the party, you need to spend some time thinking about the proper foods and drinks you'll provide and make a list. Then go shopping several days before the party so that you can have everything prepared and avoid being in a hurry or in a mess on the day of the party.

Eighth, check again on the night before the party. Make sure everything is OK, such as whether there is an area for guests' coats, whether there are enough plates and seats, whether there are extra soap and clean hand towel in the bathroom, etc.

Ninth, dress up early and greet your guests in person. Some guests may arrive early, so you'd better set aside enough time to dress up. Besides, to show your sincerity and kindness, you need to greet all the guests in person and try to make them feel easy and comfortable.

Finally, try to mingle with the guests and enjoy the party. While making an effort to entertain other guests and pull off the party, you can grasp every chance to enjoy the fun of it. Your attention and participation can always leave a good impression to the guests.

Read the passage aloud, and decide whether the following statements are true or false. Write T for true and F for false.

1) _____ It is not necessary to set a theme for your party.
2) _____ You should plan your party carefully to avoid unexpected consequences.
3) _____ Usually you need to send out invitations four or six weeks in advance so that the guests may have time to consider and rearrange their schedules.
4) _____ The most important thing you should take into consideration when decorating the venue of the party is safety and security.
5) _____ It is not necessary to check again on the night before the party if you think you have made a good preparation.

Chapter 10

Foods and Drinks
餐饮酒水

Focus on Learning 学习要点

- 旅游会话　　Taking an Order for Western Food　点西餐
- 旅行故事　　Pardon Me, Ma'am　对不起，夫人
- 旅游听力　　Table Etiquette　餐桌礼仪
- 旅游视频　　Etiquette for Ordering Wine　点葡萄酒的礼仪
- 旅游阅读　　Idioms Relating to Foods and Drinks
　　　　　　　餐饮酒水相关成语
- 旅游写作　　Notice　通知
- 旅游歌曲　　Say you, Say me　说你，说我
- 知识扩展　　American Food　美国菜

Useful Words and Expressions

immigrant(移民)/ 'imigrənt/: a person who migrates to another country, usually for permanent residence

taco(墨西哥煎玉米卷)/ 'tɑ:kəu/: Mexican cookery. An often crisply fried tortilla folded over and filled, as with seasoned chopped meat, lettuce, tomatoes, and cheese

boast(以有……而自豪)/bəust/: to be proud in the possession of something

savory(风味极佳的)/ 'seivəri/: pleasant or agreeable in taste or smell

gourmet(美食家)/ 'guəmei/: a connoisseur of fine food and drink

cutlery(刀具)/ 'kʌtləri/: cutting instruments collectively, esp. knives for cutting food

beverage(饮料)/ 'bevə ridʒ/: any potable liquid, esp. one other than water, as tea, coffee, beer, or milk

main course(主菜): the principal dish of a meal

dessert(甜食)/di'zə:t/: cake, pie, fruit, pudding, ice cream, etc. served as the final course of a meal

clam(蛤蜊)/klæm/: any of various bivalve mollusks, esp. certain edible species

chowder(杂烩)/ 'tʃaudə/: a thick soup or stew made of clams, fish, or vegetables, with potatoes, onions, and other ingredients and seasonings

Chapter 10 Foods and Drinks 餐饮酒水

Speaking for Travel
旅游会话

I. Dialogue

Taking an Order for Western Food 点西餐

1. Listen to the situational dialogue carefully, and match the information in column A with that in column B.

Column A	Column B
1) main course	A. sparkling mineral water
2) salad	B. a bowl of clam chowder, a wild salmon
3) drink	C. a chocolate cake
4) dessert after meal	D. a mixed fruit salad
5) extra service	E. a bucket of ice

2. Listen to the situational dialogue again, repeat it sentence by sentence, and then role play it in pairs.

Waiter: Good evening, sir. Here is our menu. Would you like something to drink before your order?

Tom: Yes, sparkling mineral water, please.

Waiter: No problem. Are you ready to order now, or should I come back later?

Tom: I'm ready to order now.

Waiter: What would you like?

Tom: I'd like to have a bowl of clam chowder, a wild salmon.

Waiter: OK! Anything else?

Tom: And a mixed fruit salad please.

Waiter: How about some dessert after meal?

Tom: A chocolate cake, please.

Waiter: I guess that'll be enough.

Tom: Yes. Thank you.

Waiter: Let me repeat your order: a bowl of clam chowder, a wild salmon, a mixed salad and a chocolate cake. Is that right?

Tom: Yes. By the way, could you bring me a bucket of ice please?

Waiter: Sure, sir. I'll be right back to you with sparkling water and ice.

II. Story-retelling

Listen to the funny story and retell it using your own words. You may refer to the key words or phrases given in the box.

dinner	waitress	notice	slide down
unconcerned	down the chair	out of sight	unruffled
pardon	husband	reply	

Pardon Me, Ma'am 对不起，夫人

A man and a beautiful woman were having dinner in a fine restaurant. Their waitress, taking another order at a table a few paces away suddenly noticed that the man was slowly sliding down his chair and under the table, but the woman acted unconcerned. The waitress watched as the man slid all the way down his chair and out of sight under the table. Still, the woman dining across from him appeared calm and unruffled, apparently unaware that her dining companion had

Chapter 10 Foods and Drinks 餐饮酒水

disappeared. After the waitress finished taking the order, she came over to the table and said to the woman, "Pardon me, ma'am, but I think your husband just slid under the table." The woman calmly looked up at her and replied firmly, "No he didn't. My husband just walked in the door."

Listening for Travel
旅游听力

Table Etiquette 餐桌礼仪

1. Listen to the passage twice and fill in the blanks with the information you hear (one word for one blank).

As soon as you are seated, 1)_____ the napkin from your place setting, unfold it, and put it in your 2)_____. Do not shake it open. At some very formal restaurants, the waiter may do this for the diners, but it is not 3)_____ to place your own napkin in your lap.

The napkin rests on the lap till the end of the meal. Don't clean the cutlery or 4)_____ your face with the napkin. If you excuse yourself from the table, loosely fold the napkin and place it to the left or right of your 5)_____. At the end of the meal, 6)_____ the napkin semi-folded at the left side of the place setting.

Eat to your left, drink to your right. Any food dish to the left is yours, and any 7)_____ to the right is yours. Starting with the knife, fork, or spoon that is 8)_____ from your plate, work your way in, using one 9)_____ for each course. The salad fork is on your outermost left, followed by your dinner fork. Your soup spoon is on your outermost right, followed by your beverage spoon, salad knife and dinner knife. Your 10)_____ spoon and fork are

123

English for Tourism

above your plate or brought out with dessert. If you remember the rule to work from the outside in, you'll be fine.

2. Orally summarize the main ideas of the above passage and write them down on the following lines.

1) _____
2) _____
3) _____

Watching for Travel 旅游视频

Etiquette for Ordering Wine 点葡萄酒的礼仪

Brief information from the video:

The primary purpose of ordering wine is to ensure you get a suitable pairing between your entree and the wine. Do not be afraid to ask the waiter or sommelier for advice.

Verify that it is in fact the wine that you order not just the name of the wine, but also the vintage. The same wine can be different prices depending on the vintage.

Once the waiter shows you the wine and you agree that this is the wine you in fact selected. They will go ahead and uncork the wine and he shoots up the cork on the table. Now, don't go and smell the cork as it's not going to give you any value, it is just going to smell like cork, but what you can do is to look at the cork and deduce whether or not, the cork is tinted or the wine maybe tinted based on cork discoloration.

Swirl, sniff and taste the wine. The point of tasting the wine is just to ensure

Chapter 10　Foods and Drinks 餐饮酒水

that it is not spoiled or corked. Once you tell the waiter that you accept the wine, the waiter will go clock wise around the table to your party and fill each person's glass, ladies first. As the host, your glass will be topped off last.

Watch the short video twice, and complete the following requirements.

Step 1: Divide the class into groups, and ask each student to take a note of what they have watched or heard. Compare the notes with their teammates.

Step 2: Make a brief summary of steps to order wine in a restaurant according to the video.

Summary:

1) _____
2) _____
3) _____
4) _____
5) _____

Idioms Relating to Foods and Drinks 餐饮酒水相关成语

1. **Survey:** Take this fun quiz to find out a number of common expressions which are derived from food and drink items.

1) My brother's car is really souped up. Which sentence best describes his car? (　　)

　　A. The car runs on soup instead of petrol

English for Tourism

B. The car is very powerful

C. The car is in the garage getting fixed

D. It's a very old car

2) What do we mean when we say something is a piece of cake? (   )

A. It is the only answer

B. It is only part of a problem

C. It is easy

D. It is difficult

3) What would you call someone who spends a lot of time watching TV and eating junk food? (   )

A. a sofa king   B. a couch potato

C. a sweet potato   D. a suite potato

4) My grandfather says I am the apple of his eye. What did he mean? (   )

A. I am his favorite grandchild   B. He thinks I like apples

C. He wants me to buy him apples   D. He thinks I am very sweet

5) My friend is very energetic, she can't sit still. I could say she (   )

A. has had one too many beans   B. has too many beans

C. is full of beans   D. needs more beans

6) If I want to summarize something, which phrase can I use to begin the summary? (   )

A. Here's the nutcase

B. To nut the shell

C. The nut of the matter is…

D. In a nutshell…

Chapter 10　Foods and Drinks 餐饮酒水

> **Word Tips**
> soup up:　　加大(汽车)的马力　　petrol:　　汽油
> garage:　　车库；汽车修理站　　junk:　　无价值的东西
> energetic:　　精力充沛的　　　　summarize:　　总结

2. Discuss: What are similarities and differences between food in American culture and Chinese culture?

"Tell me what you eat, and I'll tell you who you are," wrote renowned gastronome Jean Anthelme Brillat-Savarin in 1825. Everyone eats; but what we eat, where and how we eat, and with whom we eat: these are matters of culture.

Lead-in questions:

1) What are some elements that the Chinese and American diets have in common?

2) What influence does America has on the Chinese diet?

3) What influence does China has on the American diet?

4) In your opinion, Which country has a healthier diet, America or China? Why?

Group Work: What are similarities and differences between food in American culture and Chinese culture?

Step 1: Divide the class into groups.

Step 2: Ask students to discuss in details on the above questions and summarize the similarities and differences between food in American culture and Chinese culture.

Step 3: Have some groups give their presentations in front of the class.

English for Tourism

Writing for Travel 旅游写作

Notice 通知

Read the notice about account settlement in the hotel. Make a dialogue between the guest and the cashier.

NOTICE

Dear Guest,

The hotel does not subscribe to credit cards. As a registered guest, you may settle your account by cash, traveler's checks or personal check. For your convenience, counter checks are available.

When settling your account, please remind the cashier of recent charges such as room service or gratuities which may not have reached the counter. This will avoid a late charge billing after your departure.

Thanks.

Robert Smith

General Manger

Chapter 10 Foods and Drinks 餐饮酒水

Singing for Travel
旅游歌曲

Say you, Say me 说你，说我

Lionel Richie

1. Singing English songs together with tourists can stimulate their interest, and liven up the atmosphere when they travel. Listen to the song casually with reference to the lyrics.

Say you, say me

Say it for always

That's the way it should be

Say you, say me

Say it together, naturally

I had a dream

I had an awesome dream

People in the park

Playing games in the dark

And what they played

Was a masquerade

But from behind the walls of doubt

A voice was crying out

Say you, say me.

Say it for always

That's the way it should be

Say you, say me

Say it together, naturally

As we go down

Life's lonesome highway

Seems the hardest thing to do

Is to find a friend or two

That helping hand

Someone who understands

And when you feel You've lost your ways

You've got someone there to say

I'll show you

Say you, say me

Say it for always

That's the way it should be

English for Tourism

Say you, say me

Say it together, naturally

So you think you know the answers

Oh, no!

Well, the world's got you dancing

That's right, I'm telling you

It's time to start believing

Oh, yes!

Believe in who you are

You are a shining star

Say you ,say me

Say it for always

That's the way it should be

Say you ,say me

Say it together, naturally

Say it together, naturally.

2. One student role plays a tour guide while others act as tourists. Sing and enjoy the English song together.

Additional Know-how
知识扩展

American Food 美国菜

What we eat reflects who we are—as people and as a culture. When you think about what is "American food". At first you might think the answer is as easy as pie. To many people, American food means hamburgers, hot dogs, fried chicken and pizzaas. If you have a "sweet tooth," you might even think of apple pies or chocolate chip cookies. It's true that Americans do eat those things. But are those the only kind of food you can find in America?

Except for Thanksgiving turkey, it's hard to find a typical "American" food. The United States is a land of immigrants. So Americans eat food from many

Chapter 10 Foods and Drinks 餐饮酒水

different countries. When people move to America, they bring their cooking styles with them. That's why you can find almost every kind of ethnic food in America. In some cases, Americans have adopted foods from other countries as favorites. Americans love Italian pizzas, Mexican tacos and Chinese egg rolls. But the American version doesn't taste quite like the original.

As with any large country, the USA has several distinct regions. Each region boasts its own special style of food. In the South you can enjoy country-style cooking. If your journey through Louisiana, you can try some spicy Cajun cuisine. In New England you can taste sample savory seafood dishes. While traveling through the Midwest, "the breadbasket of the nation", you may enjoy the delicious baked goods. In the Southwest you can try some tasty Tex-Mex treats. Then you can finish your food tour in the Pacific Northwest with some gourmet coffee.

Americans living at a fast pace often just "grab a quick bite." Fast food restaurants offer people on the run everything from fried chicken to fried rice. Microwave dinners and instant foods make cooking at home a snap. Of course, one of the most common quick American meals is sandwich. If it can fit between two slices of bread, Americans probably make a sandwich out of it. Peanut butter and jelly is an all-time American favorite.

English for Tourism

American culture is a good illustration of the saying "you are what you eat". Americans represent a wide range of backgrounds and ways of thinking. The variety of foods in the USA reflects the diversity of personal tastes. The food may be international or regional. Sometimes it's fast, and sometimes it's not so fast. It might be junk food, or natural food. In any case, the style is all-American.

Read the passage aloud, and decide whether the following statements are true or false. Write T for true and F for false.

1) _____ Thanksgiving turkey is not a typical "American" food.
2) _____ You can find almost every kind of ethnic food in America.
3) _____ Americans love Italian pizzas, Mexican tacos and Chinese egg rolls because the American version tastes exactly like the original.
4) _____ Peanut butter and jelly is an all-time American favorite.
5) _____ The variety of foods in the USA reflects the diversity of personal tastes.

Chapter 11

Footing the Bill
付账买单

Focus on Learning 学习要点

- 旅游会话   A Miscalculated Bill 账单出错
- 旅行故事   The Bill 账单
- 旅游听力   ABC about Tipping in the USA 美国小费常识
- 旅游视频   How to Tip in a Restaurant? 怎样在饭店付小费?
- 旅游阅读   Who will pay 谁来付钱
- 旅游歌曲   Let It Be 由它去
- 知识扩展   Tips for Paying the Bill 结账小窍门

Useful Words and Expressions

owing to(因为): because of; due to

hint(暗示)/hint/: to make indirect suggestion or allusion; subtly imply

intend(打算)/in'tend/: to have in mind as something to be done or brought about; plan

in addition(另外): as well as; besides

thoughtful(周到的)/'θɔːtful/: showing consideration for others; considerate

occupy(占有)/'ɔkjupai/: to be in a place

split(均分)/split/: to divide between two or more persons, groups, etc.; share

pick up(支付): to be prepared to pay

tab(账单)/tæb/: a bill, esp. for a meal or drinks; the whole cost of something

embarrass(使尴尬)/im'bærəs/: to cause confusion and shame to; make uncomfortably self-conscious; disconcert; abash

convenience(方便)/kən'viːnjəns/: the quality of being convenient; suitability

proportion(部分)/prə'pɔːʃən/: a portion or part in its relation to the whole

encounter(遇到)/in'kauntə/: to meet with

superior(上等的)/sjuː'piəriə/: of higher grade or quality

profession(职业)/prə'feʃən/: any vocation or business

porter(行李员)/'pɔːtə/: a person hired to carry burdens or baggage, as at a railroad station or a hotel

Chapter 11　Footing the Bill 付账买单

Speaking for Travel 旅游会话

I. Dialogue

A Miscalculated Bill 账单出错

1. Listen to the situational dialogue carefully, and match the information in column A with that in column B.

Column A	Column B
1) total of the check	A. not included
2) overcharged amount	B. the cashier
3) alcohol ordered	C. $110
4) person responsible for the mistake	D. $30
5) service charge	E. whisky

2. Listen to the situational dialogue again, repeat it sentence by sentence, and then role play it in pairs.

Mike:　Waiter. May I have the check please?

Waiter: Yes, sir. It is right here. It totals $110.

Mike:　Let me see. Excuse me. What's this 30 dollars for?

Waiter: It is for the shrimp combo.

Mike:　But I didn't order that. I just had a steak dinner, a vegetable soup, some onion rings and a cup of whisky.

English for Tourism

Waiter: I'm sorry, sir, just a moment. I'll check it for you.

(A few minutes later)

I'm awfully sorry. The cashier miscalculated the bill. Here is the changed bill. Could you check again?

Mike: That's all right. Does this include the service charge?

Waiter: No, sir.

Mike: Here is $100. Keep the change, please.

Waiter: Thank you, sir. Welcome to our restaurant again.

Mike: I will. Thank you. Bye.

Waiter: Bye.

II. Story-retelling

Listen to the funny story and retell it using your own words. You may refer to the key words or phrases given in the box.

beer	serves	four dollars	twenty-dollar bill
accept	ten-dollar bill	reject	singles

The Bill 账单

A man walks into a bar and says, "Excuse me. I'd like a pint of beer".

The bartender serves the drink and says, "That'll be four dollars".

The customer pulls out a twenty-dollar bill and hands it to the bartender.

"Sorry, sir", the bartender says, "but I can't accept that".

The man pulls out a ten-dollar bill and the bartender rejects his money again.

"What's going on here?" the man asks.

Pointing to a neon sign, the bartender explains, "This is a Singles Bar".

Chapter 11 Footing the Bill 付账买单

Listening for Travel 旅游听力

ABC about Tipping in the USA 美国小费常识

1. Listen to the passage twice and fill in the blanks with the information you hear (one word for one blank).

In the United States there are a few 1)_____ where tipping is expected. The one you will encounter most often is at restaurants. American restaurants do not add a service 2)_____ to the bill. Therefore it is 3)_____ that the customer will leave a tip for the server. Common 4)_____ is to leave a tip that is 5)_____ to 15% of the total bill for acceptable service, and about 20% for superior service. If the service was unusually poor, then you could leave a smaller tip, about 6)_____.

Other professions where 7)_____ is expected include hairdressers, taxi drivers, hotel porters, parking valets, and bartenders. The 8)_____ rule is to tip about 15% of the bill. In situations where there is no bill (as with hotel porters and parking valets), the tip may 9)_____ from $1 to $5, depending on the 10)_____ of establishment and how good the service was.

2. Orally summarize the main ideas of the above passage and write them down on the following lines.

1) _____
2) _____
3) _____

English for Tourism

Watching for Travel
旅游视频

How to Tip in a Restaurant? 怎样在饭店付小费？

Brief information from the video:

Tipping is the easy way to reward a waiter who helps you to have an enjoyable meal. But rules vary depending on the situation and level of service.

Evaluate Service: When deciding how much you should leave for a tip, thinking about your overall enjoyment of the meal and how or if the waiting staff has contributed to it.

The average tip: 10% of the final bill is a nominal amount you should tip. This may vary depending on the quality of service and is a sliding scale from 0% to 25%.

When to give a big tip: There are several occasions when leaving a larger tip than 10% is appropriate and could be anything up to 40%. If the service is unusually helpful, friendly and unobtrusive, if your waiter has been particularly knowledgeable about the food and wine, if your waiter has gone out of their way to accommodate an unusual request or problem, or if you are a large group of six or over.

When to leave a small tip: If the waiter has done less than the bare minimum and has been generally unhelpful, also if the waiter gets the order wrong or doesn't pay attention to special requirements and food allergies, if a waiter is actually rude or abusive to a customer.

When to leave no tip at all: Reserve 0% tips for venues to which you never wish to return as you may find it difficult to get a table once you've made known your disappointment.

Chapter 11　Footing the Bill　付账买单

Included discretionary tip: Increasingly restaurants are choosing to include a discretionary or optional charge with the final bill which can vary from about 12% to 15%. If the service doesn't live up to their suggested tip, then don't be embarrassed to remove it.

Tipping by card: This is a simple and discreet way of tipping but bear in mind that the restaurant may use that tip as a contribution to its waiting staff's wages. To ensure that the waiter actually receives all of the tip, it may be best to leave it for them in cash.

Tipping in cash: Once you have paid the bill, leave the desired amount on the table in a neat pile, or a bill wallet left on the table. Never thrust money into the waiter's hand during the meal or as you leave as it could potentially be embarrassing for the waiter. If you don't have the correct change for a tip, don't be embarrassed about asking your waiter to break a note.

In a hurry: If you are in a hurry and are paying for your bill and service in cash, it is acceptable to pay the waiter for the meal with enough excess to cover his tip and immediately leave.

Watch the short video twice, and complete the following requirements.

Step 1: Divide the class into groups, and ask each student to take a note of what they have watched or heard. Compare the notes with their teammates.

Step 2: Make a brief summary of ways to tip a waiter according to the video.

Summary:

1) _____
2) _____
3) _____
4) _____
5) _____

English for Tourism

Reading for Travel 旅游阅读

The Bills on Who 谁来付钱

1. Listen to the passage and decide whether the following statements are true or false. Write T for true and F for false.

You and your friends just enjoyed a fantastic dinner party when the bill arrives. At that moment, conversations and libations come to a sudden halt. Did someone order an awkward silence? Below are a few tips for hosts and guests to help avoid the sticky situations that can come with the check.

If you're a host:

If you're vehemently opposed to having your guests pay, then consider your budget when choosing a venue. Cooking a meal for a dinner party at your house will certainly be less expensive than footing an entire restaurant bill. Whatever venue you select, be sure to mention that the meal and drinks will be your treat so guests know what to expect.

Decide what role you'd like to play in the party. If you'd like to be the sole host, and then understand that you'll be responsible for the check at the end of the night. Adding a few co-hosts is an easy way to share the party expenses.

If you'd like your guests to chip in, let them know beforehand. There are plenty of polite, tactful ways to go about this. For example, add a gentle reminder to your invitation such as, "Separate checks will be provided." This

Chapter 11   Footing the Bill 付账买单

gets the point across that everyone will pay for what they get without having to say it directly.

If you have arranged a set price with the restaurant, it is acceptable to ask guests to contribute a per-person charge. Just let them know what they'll be getting for their money. "The cost will be $35 per person, which includes drinks, appetizer, entree, dessert, tax and tip." But be fair and honest—don't ask for more than the actual price to "pay for your efforts".

If you're a guest:

If it hasn't been addressed, feel free to ask your host if he or she is expecting guests chip in. Asking whether or not the restaurant will accept credit cards is one way of finding out your host's intentions without looking overly concerned about money.

So the check arrives and the host decides to split the bill evenly among all the guests. This works well for simplicity's sake, but not for your budget-conscious ordering. Let your host know beforehand that you'll be ordering light (you can always say you had a big lunch if you don't want to attribute it to thrift). If the host knows, he or she can speak up on your behalf.

If you're a guest who orders a five-course meal plus cocktails, it's kind to offer to pay a little extra to cover the difference. Or if you notice a guest who is clearly getting the short end of the stick, maybe say something diplomatic like, "I don't think everyone had cocktails and desserts, so perhaps we should just pay for what we ordered".

  1) _____ As a host, you should tell your guests that the meal and drinks will be your treat if you are opposed to having your guests pay.

  2) _____ You should not add co-hosts to share the party expenses.

  3) _____ If you would like to have the guests share the expense, you should let them know beforehand.

4) _____ You can ask for more than the actual price to pay for your efforts.

5) _____ If you are a guest, you'd better ask the host if he is expecting to split the bill.

6) _____ One of the ways to know the intention of the host is to ask whether the restaurant will take credit card or not.

7) _____ It has been a long practice to split the bill evenly among the guests.

8) _____ If you order more food than other guests, you'd better pay a little more to cover the difference.

Word Tips

libation:	敬酒	fantastic:	非常出色的
halt:	停止	sticky:	为难的
vehemently:	激烈地	venue:	举行场所
sole:	唯一的	tactful:	机智的
contribute:	贡献	attribute to:	把……归因于
thrift:	节约	diplomatic:	有外交手腕的
foot the bill:	付账		

2. Discuss: If your friends ask you to dine out in a restaurant, who do you think should pay the bill?

While dinning out is pleasant and palatable, paying the bill is always hard to deal with. Sometimes you and your friends may fight to pay the bill, which always makes a big scene and leaves all of you embarrassed. So, it is important to make clear who will pay the bill before you dine out with your friends.

Chapter 11　Footing the Bill 付账买单

Lead-in Questions:

1) If nothing is addressed, do you think the person who asks you to dine out should pay the bill?

2) Do you think boys instead of girls should pay the bill?

3) If you order less than other friends, do you think it is unfair to split the bill evenly?

4) Do you think it is polite to just pay for what you ordered?

5) What do you think about the saying "Go Dutch"?

Group Work: If your friends ask you to dine out in a restaurant, who do you think should pay the bill?

Step 1: Divide the class into groups.

Step 2: Ask students to discuss in details on the above questions and summarize who should pay the bill if their friends ask them to dine out in a restaurant. Give sufficient reasons.

Step 3: Have some groups give their presentations in front of the class.

Let It Be 由它去
The Beatles

1. Singing English songs together with tourists can stimulate their interest, and liven up the atmosphere when they travel. Listen to the song casually with reference to the lyrics.

English for Tourism

When I find myself in times of trouble

Mother Mary comes to me

Speaking words of wisdom, let it be

And in my hour of darkness

She is standing right in front of me

Speaking words of wisdom, let it be

Let it be, let it be

Let it be, let it be

Whisper words of wisdom, let it be

And when the broken hearted people

Living in the world agree

There will be an answer, let it be

For though they may be parted

There is still a chance that they will see

There will be an answer, let it be

Let it be, let it be

Let it be, let it be

Yeah there will be an answer, let it be

Let it be, let it be

Let it be, let it be

Whisper words of wisdom, let it be

Let it be, let it be

Ah let it be, yeah let it be

Whisper words of wisdom, let it be

And when the night is cloudy

There is still a light that shines on me

Shine on until tomorrow, let it be

I wake up to the sound of music,

Mother Mary comes to me

Speaking words of wisdom, let it be

Yeah let it be, let it be

Let it be, yeah let it be

Oh there will be an answer, let it be

Let it be, let it be

Let it be, yeah let it be

Whisper words of wisdom, let it be

2. One student role plays a tour guide while others act as tourists. Sing and enjoy the English song together.

Chapter 11 Footing the Bill 付账买单

Additional Know-how 知识扩展

Tips for Paying the Bill 结账小窍门

It seems rather simple and easy to pay your bill in a restaurant. You can just call the waiter and tell him that you would like to pay the bill. When he gives you the bill, you should check it carefully to see whether there are any mistakes or not and make the payment if everything is all right. And then you should put some tip on the table before leaving. The whole process can be finished in several minutes if there is no problem. However, things do not always go so smoothly. Owing to these or those problems, paying the bill can be full of troubles unless you pay attention to the following tips:

Ask for your check immediately when you finish your meal because the waiter may not notice that you are through. After all, he has to take care of several tables at the same time. Besides, he doesn't want to continuously bother you to see whether you have finished or not. But making you wait for him is also something he is unwilling to do.

When you pay in cash or by credit card, you'd better put them a little out of the check presenter, and then place it on the edge of the table so as to hint the waiter that you are ready to pay the bill.

Even though you are intended to sit there chatting with your friend for a while when you are finished, you'd better tell the waiter and pay first. For one thing, he has to wait for all of his receipts being calculated before leaving. If you are the last table he serves and you delay paying the bill, he has to wait. For another, if he wants to leave, he can go after making sure whether you need anything else and arranging for another waiter to look after you.

In addition, it's thoughtful of you to give a little more tip to the waiter if you occupied the table for a long time because he earns money only by turning the limited number of tables he serves.

When you dine with several friends, you need to let the waiter know in advance whether you are going to split the bill according to what each person orders or you are going to pick up the tab for the whole table. This may help to speed up the payment process and avoid the embarrassing situation in which everyone fights over who will pay the bill.

You can usually pay the bill in three ways: cash, check and credit card. If you pay in cash, you'd better use the smallest bills you have and let the waiter know whether you need the change or not. However, when you give tip to the waiter, you should not use many small changes. If you pay with your check, first you need to ask whether check is accepted or not. If it is accepted, you should leave your home phone number and address or any other useful information for the convenience of both sides. If you pay by credit card, it's better to give tip in cash because some restaurants will take a certain proportion of the tips paid by credit card.

Read the passage aloud, and decide whether the following statements are true or false. Write T for true and F for false.

1) _____ You should ask for your check immediately when you finish your meal because the waiter may not notice that you are through.

2) _____ You should never sit there chatting with your friend when you are finished.

3) _____ You'd better give a little more tip to the waiter if you occupy the table for a long time.

4) _____ It's not necessary to tell your waiter in advance whether you will split the bill or not.

5) _____ When you give tip to the waiter, you should not use many small changes.

Chapter 12

Cruise Travel
邮轮旅游

Focus on Learning 学习要点

- 旅游会话　　Ready for Getting Aboard the Ship 准备登船
- 旅行故事　　God Could Not Save Me 上帝救不了我
- 旅游听力　　The Cabins of a Liner 邮轮舱位
- 旅游视频　　How to Cut Down the Costs for Cruise Travel? 如何减少邮轮旅行开支？
- 旅游阅读　　Water Excursions at Cancun 坎昆水上旅游
- 旅游写作　　Tour Itineraries 旅游线路
- 旅游歌曲　　Upside down 颠倒
- 知识扩展　　Cruise Vacation 邮轮度假

Useful Words and Expressions

cabin(船舱)/ˈkæbin/: an apartment or room in a ship, as for passengers

cruise(邮轮)/kruːz/: a pleasure voyage on a ship, usually with stops at various ports

all-inclusive(费用全包的): including everything; comprehensive

fascinating(迷人的/醉人的)/ˈfæsineitiŋ/: having strong charm or attraction

intimate(亲密的)/ˈintimit/: close and familiar

stroll(漫步)/strəul/: go for a quiet and unhurried walk

chapel(基督教礼堂)/ˈtʃæpəl/: place used for Christian worship

amenity(便利设施/生活福利设施)/əˈmiːniti/: a feature that makes a place pleasant, comfortable or easy to live in

penthouse(楼顶房屋)/ˈpenthaus/: apartment built on the roof of a tall building

distinction(区别)/disˈtiŋkʃən/: being, keeping things different or distinct; distinguishing

debark(登岸)/diˈbɑːk/: disembark; put on shore, go on shore

pier(码头)/piə/: structure of wood, iron, etc. built out into the sea as a landing-stage; similar structure for walking on for pleasure

seasickness(晕船)/ˈsiːˌsiknis/: nausea and dizziness, sometimes accompanied by vomiting, resulting from the rocking or swaying motion of a vessel at sea

call at(停靠): enter a harbor

passage(航程)/ˈpæsidʒ/: a voyage by water from one point to another

Chapter 12　Cruise Travel 邮轮旅游

I. Dialogue

Ready for Getting Aboard the Ship 准备登船

1. Listen to the situational dialogue carefully, and match the information in column A with that in column B.

Column A	Column B
1) place for getting on the cruise	A. 19
2) time for leaving the port	B. pier 6
3) cabin number	C. not sure
4) sailing hours	D. 2
5) numbers of ports to be called at	E. 14

2. Listen to the situational dialogue again, repeat it sentence by sentence, and then role play it in pairs.

Tracy: Sam, where will we get on the cruise?

Sam: At Pier Six.

Tracy: That's not far from here. You told me that it would leave out at 2:00 p.m..

Sam: Yes. We have forty minutes to go.

(…)

Tracy: Finally we are at Pier Six for Alaska. Let's go on board.

Sam: OK. There are many passengers on board already.

Tracy: What is our cabin number?

Sam: Cabin number 19, Atlantic Deck.

Tracy: I hope that I won't suffer from seasickness.

Sam: I guess you'd better take some medicines before sailing.

Tracy: I will, just in case. How long does it take to our destination?

Sam: About 14 hours.

Tracy: How many ports do we call at on our passage to Alaska?

Sam: I'm not sure. Hey, Tracy, here is our cabin number 19, Atlantic deck…

II. Story—retelling

Listen to the funny story and retell it using your own words. You may refer to the key words or phrases given in the box.

drown	flood	ankles	fire truck	lift
save	ribs	coast guard	head	helicopter
safety	is bound to	heaven	god	

God Could Not Save Me 上帝救不了我

There was a guy named Jimmy, and his town was being drowned by a flood. When the water was around his ankles, a fire truck came by saying, "Jimmy, need a lift?" "No, no, I'm fine. God will save me." The fire truck left.

As the water reached his ribs, the Coast Guard came by saying, "Jimmy! Need a lift?" "No! God will save me!" The Coast Guard went away.

When the water had reached Jimmy's head, a helicopter flew overhead. The driver shouted, "Jimmy! Com on, I'll take you to safety!" "That's all right! God is bound to save me now!" The helicopter flew away.

Jimmy died. When he went to heaven, Jimmy asked God, "God, why didn't you save me?" God answers, "I sent you a fire truck, a coast guard, and a helicopter, what more do you want?"

Chapter 12　Cruise Travel 邮轮旅游

Listening for Travel 旅游听力

The Cabins of a Liner 邮轮舱位

1. Listen to the passage twice and fill in the blanks with the information you hear (one word for one blank).

Ticket price on a cruise ship is 1)_____ on the size, location, and amenities of your 2)_____. It also depends on the season, with holidays and summers usually more 3)_____. On the low-price end, cabins have few amenities, are 4)_____ deep in the ship, and can be as small as 100 square feet. At the high end, they're more like 5) _____ penthouses than cabins, up to thousands of square feet in size; they have great views and numerous 6)_____ touches.

Keep in mind that, once you leave your cabin, no class 7)_____ exist. In theory, it really does work this way most of the time. All passengers on a cruise ship are treated 8)_____, share the same facilities, and usually eat in the same restaurants. However, some distinctions do 9)_____. When boarding before a cruise, some Lines give higher-end occupants passes that allow them to avoid long check-in lines. Moreover, higher-end cabins usually get to leave first when 10)_____.

2. Orally summarize the main ideas of the above passage and write them down on the following lines.

1) _____
2) _____
3) _____

Watching for Travel
旅游视频

How to Cut Down the Costs for Cruise Travel?
如何减少邮轮旅行开支？

Brief information from the video:

Research and hire travel agent: Research cruise lines to find lines going to your destination. Hire a travel agent specializing in those lines. Be sure to ask about discounts.

Buy early and buy cruise-only: Buy early, in the off-season, and buy a cruise-only package without airfare since air-inclusive packages cost more.

Book a small cabin: There are so many activities on the ship that you will hardly use your room.

Be a VIP: Ask your travel agent to tell the cruise line that you are a VIP and a will-be intended frequent customer to get a free upgrade and to enjoy other special rights.

BYOB (bring your own booze): Fill plastic bottles with liquor and then use your unlimited soda sticker for mixers. Pay only a corkage fee at dinner.

Secure your own ground transport and tours: These measures will cost much less than cruise buses and tours.

Watch out for cash-guzzling extras: such as shipboard photos, bar purchases, and onboard art auctions.

Purchase next cruise: You can get a better deal as well as more credits.

Chapter 12   Cruise Travel 邮轮旅游

Watch the short video twice, and complete the following requirements.

Step 1: Divide the class into groups, and ask each student to take a note of what they have watched or heard. Compare the notes with their teammates.

Step 2: Make a brief summary of ways to save money for booking cruise according to the video.

Summary:

1) _____
2) _____
3) _____

Reading for Travel 旅游阅读

Water Excursions at Cancun 坎昆水上旅游

1. Listen to the passage and decide whether the following statements are true or false. Write T for true and F for false.

Warm white sand beaches, crystal indigo seas, romantic Caribbean nights, world-class hotels, restaurants and nightlife; sounds like a paradise? This is Cancun, a balmy tropical climate, water sports and a world resort where you could keep busy 24 hours a day with activities and tours available. However, the real purpose of Cancun is to provide you a tranquil retreat where you can relax to your hearts content along the peaceful shore of the Caribbean.

The original developers and the Mexican government can be proud of what they have accomplished so far. Built in 1972 in a location with lots of snakes and mosquitoes, with its government's Growth Pole Strategy and financing on the first 8 hotels building, Cancun has been carefully developed into one of the most

English for Tourism

polished resorts. The success of these first ventures attracts investors that help turn Cancun into the thriving resort community we see today. Below are major attractions of Cancun.

Beaches:

The beaches with powdery, incredibly white sand and incredibly warm blue water of Caribbean Sea, are Cancun's most famous attractions. The northern side and the eastern side of the city are laced with some exotic beaches where you can relax as well as join in sporty activities.

Scuba Diving:

Water sports, scuba diving and snorkeling have all become leading attractions around the resort of Cancun, along with sport fishing. Beneath the waters you'll discover a wealth of marine attractions, including beautiful coral reefs and many colorful creatures, such as dolphins. Other popular water sports include sailing, windsurfing, kayaking and even parasailing.

Dolphin Discovery:

Dolphin Discovery is one of the region's most memorable attractions and located just outside of Cancun, on the nearby Isla Mujeres. You can come here to swim with the dolphins, learn more about these highly intelligent creatures, or simply enjoy observing their play.

Yachting/Cruise:

Various cruises are available around the Cancun coastline and offer a great way to sightsee and enjoy some truly spectacular views of the city itself, along with commentary and refreshments. Boats and yachts are available for hire at the Gran Marina de Cancun you should prefer to explore the waters at your own pace.

Interactive Aquarium Cancun:

The Interactive Aquarium Cancun brings you highlights such as, large aquariums with colorful marine fish, landscaped reefs and even the occasional diver. It is possible to get up-close and personal with rays and starfish, and an unforgettable opportunity to swim and interact with friendly dolphins in an enormous pool. Moreover, you can feed the sharks from an underwater cage, visit the entertaining macaws in the bird sanctuary, enjoy a meal at the onsite restaurant, and visit the boutique gift shop, to purchase your aquarium related

Chapter 12   Cruise Travel 邮轮旅游

souvenir.

There are lots of more attractions to keep you busy.

1) _____ Cancun is a natural attractive tourism resort from the very beginning.

2) _____ The real purpose of Cancun is to provide you a tranquil retreat where you can relax to your heart's content.

3) _____ The northern side and the eastern side of the city are laced with some exotic beaches where you can relax but can't join in sporty activities.

4) _____ By scuba diving, you can discover a wealth of marine attractions and many colorful creatures.

5) _____ If you prefer to explore the waters at your own pace, you can hire boats and yachts.

6) _____ You can feed the shark when you swim close to it.

Word Tips

indigo:	靛青色	balmy:	温暖惬意的
tropical:	热带的	tranquil:	安宁的
venture:	经营项目	thriving:	扣人心弦的
scuba diving:	戴水肺潜水	snorkeling:	带呼吸管潜水
coral beef:	珊瑚礁	windsurfing:	帆板运动
kayaking:	独木舟	parasailing:	滑翔伞
commentary:	现场解说	refreshment:	食物饮料
yacht:	快艇	aquarium:	水族馆
ray:	魟	macaw:	金刚鹦鹉
sanctuary:	鸟兽保护区	boutique:	时装店

2. Discuss: Can we take Cancun and develop our tourism in certain areas, and how?

Tourism in China has greatly expanded over the last few decades. Now China has become one of the world's most-watched and hottest outbound tourist markets, the world's fourth largest country for inbound tourism. According to the WTO, in terms of total outbound travel spending, China is currently ranked fifth and is expected to be the fastest growing in the world by 2015. Do you think that we can take Cancun and develop our tourism in certain areas and how?

Lead-in Questions:

1) What is your impression of Cancun's tourism?

2) Can you list some factors which help to boom Cancun's tourism?

3) What do you think would be important factors to develop tourism in China?

4) Is Cancun a good example for us to follow?

5) If so, where do you think would be good places to be chosen and developed?

Group Work: Can we take Cancun and develop our tourism in certain areas, and how?

Step 1: Divide the class into groups

Step 2: Ask students to discuss in details the above questions and summa- rize.

Step 3: Have some groups give their presentations in front of the class.

Tour Itineraries 旅游线路

Read the following tour itinerary and arrange a 5-day itinerary for a group in your city, and discuss it with the tour leader.

Chapter 12　Cruise Travel 邮轮旅游

A Cruising Discovery of China

Cities to visit: Hong Kong, Qingdao, Shanghai

Quotation: US $2500/p.p.

Departure time: July, 2012.

Tour Description: The itinerary has been expertly planned to give you the perfect combination of cruising and touring, beginning with you're the first cruise in dazzling Hong Kong(香港). In Qiangdao(青岛), you will go boating and admire the marvel of the architectures in different styles. In Shanghai(上海), you will have a Huangpu River (黄浦江)cruise, watching both the old and the new Shanghai. The cruise in China takes you back 5000 years of the Chinese civilization, and carries you to the brink of the future of New China.

Day 01

Arrive at Hong Kong by Air China(中国国际航空公司) at 12:30 (Beijing Time), meet your guide and transfer to the Holiday Inn Hotel(假日酒店). Welcome dinner in the evening. (LD)

Day02

American buffet breakfast between 07:00-08:30, and take a bus ride to Hong Kong Ocean Park(香港海洋公园). Come back to the hotel after lunch for a short break. At 16:00, cruise around the Victoria Harbor(维多利亚港口) on the Queen Elizabeth(伊丽莎白皇后号) and tour the Causeway Bay(铜锣湾) in the evening. (BLD)

Day 03

Finish your breakfast, and leave your checkout luggage out of your room at 07:30. Check out of the hotel before 08:30. Take a flight to Qingdao, and transfer to the Qingdao Shangri-la Hotel(青岛香格里拉酒店). (BLD)

Day 04

Leave at 14:30 for the Plank Bridge(栈桥), one of the must-see tourist attractions in Qingdao. Back to hotel about 17:00, and go to watch acrobatics show while enjoying the Qingdao beer at the beach. (BLD)

Day 05

Have your breakfast and check out of hotel before 08:30, leave for the first bathing beach in Qingdao, where you may go boating or dive into the sea to explore the fantastic sea world. At 14:00, tour the Badaguan(八大关) and enjoy the old buildings which present you various architectural styles that are totally different from those of China. (BLD)

Day 06

Breakfast between 07:30-8:30. Take a fight to Shanghai, and transfer to Shanghai Jingjiang Hotel(上海锦江宾馆). After lunch, have a traditional tourist item in Shanghai- Huangpu River Cruise. In the evening, have a dinner at the top restaurant of the 468-m tall Oriental Pearl TV Tower(东方明珠电视塔) while watching the wonderful night of Shanghai. (BLD)

Day 07

Chinese breakfast between 07:00-08:30, and take a walk at the Bund(外滩) after breakfast. At 9:00, go sightseeing at Nanjing Road(南京路) which gives you a joyful and relaxed shopping atmosphere. Back to the hotel at 16:00 and get ready with luggage and carry-on before 16:45. Take a flight to San Francisco(旧金山). (BL)

Singing for Travel 旅游歌曲

Upside down 颠倒

A-Teens

1. Singing English songs together with tourists can stimulate their interest, and liven up the atmosphere when they travel. Listen to the song casually with reference to the lyrics.

My grades are down from A's to D's
I'm way behind in history
I lost myself in fantasies

Of you and me together
I don't know why-I-I but dreaming's
all I do

Chapter 12　Cruise Travel 邮轮旅游

I won't get by-I-I on mere imagination

Upside down
Bouncing off the ceiling
Inside out
Stranger to this feeling
Got no clue what I should do
But I'll go crazy if I can't get next to you

My teacher says to concentrate
So what-his name was Peter the Great
The kings and queens will have to wait
Cause I don't have forever
I wish that I-I-I could walk right up to you
Each time I try-I-I the same old hesitation
Upside down
Bouncing off the ceiling
Inside out
Stranger to this feeling

Got no clue what I should to
But I'll go crazy if I can't get next to you
Somehow someday
You will love me too
One day will be the day when all my dreams come true

Upside down
Bouncing off the ceiling
Inside out
Stranger to this feeling
Got no clue what I should do
But I'll go crazy if I can't get next to

Upside down
Bouncing off the ceiling
Inside out
Stranger to this feeling
Got no clue what I should to
But I'll go crazy if I can't get next to you

2. One student role plays a tour guide while others act as tourists. Sing and enjoy the English song together.

Cruise Vacation 邮轮度假

　　Cruise vacation is one of the most pleasurable, relaxing, fantastic vacations imaginable. Nowadays more and more people take cruise vacation because cruise

159

can help you get rid of pressures and strains of contemporary life ashore. It can also offer a means of escape from reality.

Cruise is like a self-contained floating resort that brings you to many destinations. It is a combination of adventure, excitement, romance and wonder. Once onboard, everything is taken care of. Cruising is about exploring the world. Whether you want to try new food, do something you've never done before, or see someplace you've never seen before, cruising brings out the explorer in all of you. And it offers something for all ages and interests: organized activities for children, entertainment options, gambling for adults, fitness equipment & classes, full-service spas and a variety of formal and casual dining to suit all tastes.

Compared with most land based vacations, cruising has great value and is relatively inexpensive. All-inclusive price includes: accommodations, meals, entertainment and most shipboard activities. On a cruise, you will visit a number of fascinating ports to see different sceneries and places.

Cruising is also the ideal setting for romance, intimate dinners for two, strolling on the decks at sunset and dancing the night away under the stars. Many couples tend to have their wedding onboard ships. There are some cruise lines specializing in wedding onboard and having a Wedding Chapel onboard the ship for receptions. Sailing the open seas would be a wonderful way to spend honeymoon!

Read the passage aloud, and decide whether the following statements are true or false. Write T for true and F for false.

1) _____ People take cruise due to its power to eliminate pressures and strains of contemporary life ashore.

2) _____ Cruise vacation is the most pleasurable, relaxing, fantastic vacations imaginable.

3) _____ Cruise only offers lots of casual dinning to suit all tastes.

4) _____ Cruising is more expensive than most land based vacations.

5) _____ Not all cruise lines specialize in wedding on board.

Chapter 13

Travel Abroad
国外旅游

Focus on Learning 学习要点

- 旅游会话　　Walking in the Wall Street 漫步华尔街
- 旅行故事　　The Same Good Fortune 同样好运
- 旅游听力　　An Unforgettable Trip to Niagara Falls
　　　　　　尼亚加拉瀑布难忘之旅
- 旅游视频　　Travel Guide-Ottawa 旅游指南：渥太华
- 旅游阅读　　Discover Toronto 发现多伦多
- 旅游歌曲　　Breathless 无法呼吸
- 知识扩展　　Bus Tour in New York 纽约观光车

Useful Words and Expressions

landmark(地标)/ˈlændmɑːk/: a prominent or conspicuous object on land that serves as a guide

explore(探险)/iksˈplɔː/: traverse or range over a region, area for the purpose of discovery

witness(见证)/ˈwitnis/: see, hear or know by personal presence and perception

commercial(商业性的)/kəˈməːʃəl/: prepared or acting with sole or chief emphasis on salability, profit

approximate(大约的)/əˈprɔksimeit/: near or approaching a certain state, condition

complimentary(免费赠送)/ˌkɔmpliˈment(ə)ri/: something given or supplied without charge as lodging, transportation or meals especially as an inducement to prospective customers.

inauguration(就职典礼)/iˌnɔːgjuˈreiʃən/: the action to induct into office with formal ceremonies

charge(猛攻)/tʃɑːdʒ/: to attack by rushing violently against

aggressive(有闯劲的)/əˈgresiv/: emphasizing maximum growth and capital gains over quality, security, and income

optimism(乐观主义)/ˈɔptimizəm/: a disposition or tendency to look on the more favorable side of events or conditions and to expect the most favorable outcome

prosperity(繁荣)/prɔsˈperiti/: a successful, flourishing, or thriving condition, esp. in financial

Chapter 13　Travel Abroad 国外旅游

Speaking for Travel 旅游会话

I. Dialogue

Walking in the Wall Street 漫步华尔街

1. Listen to the situational dialogue carefully, and match the information in column A with that in column B.

Column A	Column B
1) place to visit	A. a narrow street
2) the building time	B. the New York Stock Exchange
3) traveler's impression of the street	C. 26 Wall Street
4) location of Federal Hall	D. Wall Street
5) name of the right-sided building	E. 1914

2. Listen to the situational dialogue again, repeat it sentence by sentence, and then role play it in pairs.

Jack:　What are the best places to visit here?

Guide:　It depends. Since you asked about the financial center of New York, you might like to go to Wall Street.

Jack:　Good idea! Let's visit there first.

Guide:　(…) We are now at Wall Street. It was built in 1914. It runs east from Broadway to South Street on the East River, through the historical center of the Financial District. 23 Wall Street was known as the "House of Morgan".

163

English for Tourism

Jack:　Oh, it is just a narrow street. I can't imagine how it becomes the financial center in the world.

Guide: Federal Hall, located 26 Wall Street, was the site of Washington's inauguration as the first President in 1789. The present building was built in 1842.

Jack:　Does it serve as first US Customs House?

Guide: Yes. Look at that building on your right side. It is the first permanent home of the New York Stock Exchange. Several major US stock and other exchanges such as NYSE, NASDAQ, AMEX etc. remain headquartered on Wall Street and in the Financial District.

Jack:　No wonder it's the global financial center. Would you please take a photo for me?

Guide: With pleasure.

II. Story-retelling

Listen to the funny story and retell it using your own words. You may refer to the key words or phrases given in the box.

tour	complain	late afternoon	good luck	rub
clean	tomorrow	shout	kiss	buttock

The Same Good Fortune 同样好运

A group of people was touring New York. One of the women in the group was constantly complaining. The bus seats are uncomfortable. The food is terrible. It's too hot. It's too cold. The accommodations are awful.

The group arrived at the site of the famous Wall Street Bull in the late afternoon. "Good luck will be following you all your years if you rub the head of Wall Street Bull," the guide said. "Unfortunately, it's being cleaned today and so no one will be able to rub it. Perhaps we can come back tomorrow."

Chapter 13 Travel Abroad 国外旅游

"We can't be here tomorrow," the nasty woman shouted, "We have some other boring tours to go on. So I guess we can't rub the stupid Bull."

"Well now," the guide said, "it is said that if you kiss someone who has rubbed the Bull, you'll have the same good fortune."

"And I suppose you've rubbed the head of the Bull," the woman scoffed.

"No, ma'am," the frustrated guide said, "but I've rubbed its buttocks."

Listening for Travel 旅游听力

An Unforgettable Trip to Niagara Falls 尼亚加拉瀑布难忘之旅

1. Listen to the passage twice and fill in the blanks with the information you hear (one word for one blank).

Hop on a commercial airliner 1)_____ for the short flight to upstate New York, and then on to Niagara Falls by luxury motor coach! Capture 2)_____ of the beautiful New York countryside and New York City during your short flight! The experienced guides will offer expert narration with fun facts and 3)_____ about Niagara Falls.

Capture views of 4)_____ Niagara Falls from both the US and Canadian sides and spend approximately 3 hours touring each side of the Falls for an approximate 5)_____ of 6.5 hours at the Falls (time spent at the Falls varies depending on traffic, weather, etc.).

Get up close and 6)_____ with the falls on the complimentary 30-minute Maid-of-the-Mist boat excursion (May to October). This 7)_____ takes you to the base of the Canadian Falls, where you can feel the mighty force of the water as you get 8)_____! You are provided a complimentary

English for Tourism

hooded raincoat to protect against the spray of the awesome falls.

2. Orally summarize the main ideas of the above passage and write them down on the following lines.

1) _____
2) _____
3) _____

Travel Guide—Ottawa 旅游指南——渥太华

Brief information from the video:

Fourth largest city and the capital of Canada: It was chosen as such by Queen Victoria in 1857 for its strategic location as a compromise between the two colonies and their French and English population.

Extreme range of temperature: With the record high being 100 degrees Fahrenheit, the city receives roughly 93 inches of snow annually between middle December and early April. Day time temperature in January is averages 13 degrees Fahrenheit. Average temperature in July is 80 degrees Fahrenheit.

3 million visitors each year: Ottawa's Parliament Hill is home to Canada's landmark of the Parliament Buildings. The Centre Block includes the Peace Tower in national symbol. Inside the Centre Block are the House of Commerce and the Senate of Chambers and the Library of Parliament.

The Rideau Canal, a UNESCO World Heritage Site in 2007: It connects Ottawa on the Ottawa River to Kinston on Lake Ontario.

Showcase in over 300 000 tulips: Ottawa plants more of the flowers for

Chapter 13 Travel Abroad 国外旅游

capital than any of the other city.

Ottawa's Canadian Museum of Civilization: It is Canada's most visited museum tracing over a thousand years in Canadian history. The National Gallery of Canada holds the world's most comprehensive collection of Canadian and Indian arts.

The world's largest collection of huge mazes: Ottawa is with Saunders Farms housing 9 large mazes and a series of puzzle mazes.

With over 50 galleries, theaters in this area, heritage buildings, parks and shopping locations, the toughest problem for visitors in Ottawa is to decide what to do.

Watch the short video twice, and complete the following requirements.

Step 1: Divide the class into groups, and ask each student to take a note of what they have watched or heard. Compare the notes with their teammtes.

Step 2: Make a brief summary of the attractions you might visit when traveling around Ottawa according to the video.

Summary:

1) _____

2) _____

3) _____

Discover Toronto 发现多伦多

1. Listen to the passage and decide whether the following statements are true or false. Write T for true and F for false.

English for Tourism

This remarkable gem of a city is called Toronto, the capital city of Ontario, and the largest and most populated city in Canada. Toronto is on par with New York City when it comes to cultural attractions and urban endeavors.

Besides the most prominent landmark CN Tower, Royal Ontario Museum is a must-see as Canada's largest museum and one of the top ten museums in the world for natural history and world culture. It reels more than a million visitors a year. You can view mummy exhibits, Korean art and culture, bat caves and almost anything you can imagine. It boasts the largest collection of Chinese artifacts outside of Beijing and Taiwan. It is architecturally unique built during the depression era of the 1920's and recently renovated and expanded with the fusion of modern crystal/glass. Toronto is also home to a number of excellent smaller museums, focusing on subjects as such as Bata Shoe Museum, Textile Museum of Canada. Remember to take your camera with you when going around them.

If you make your way down to the waterfront, stop by Harbourfront—one of North America's largest recreational spots. With over 4 000 events annually, you'll never experience a dull moment there such as the Toronto International Film Festival; the Canadian National Exhibition. You'd better choose to view the city from one of the day/night cruises or even dine by the harbor with the beautiful night sky as your backdrop.

For visitors who like shopping, the Eaton Center located in the heart of downtown Toronto will be their paradise. It is a galleria mall featuring 320 shops and restaurants, 17 cinemas and a 400-room Marriott Hotel connected to it. The mall boasts sales of $746 per square foot of retail space—the highest in North America—and was one of the first major "downtown" shopping malls on the continent. The Eaton Center is the number one tourist attraction in Toronto with more than one million visitors a week. Another kind of shopping experience will be unforgettable in St. Jacob Farmers Market. All year long on Saturdays, you can buy anything and hassle over the price. The smell, the sites and the activity are unique. You'll see the Mennonites and Amish people with their horse and

Chapter 13　Travel Abroad 国外旅游

buggy, offering their fruits and vegetables. You can go inside the buildings and search through the unbelievable amount of stuff for sale, from Elvis pictures and brass statues to handmade wooden furniture. Groceries, antiques, sausages, livestock auctions, puppies, it is truly a unique experience.

Sports lovers must go to Hockey Hall Of Fame. Visiting the hockey hall of fame located in Brookfield place along Yonge Street would be the perfect chance for you to test your skills and knowledge of the game.

Before leaving the area, you can visit the Toronto Islands. The ferry trips across give a great view of the city skyline and the chance to take some fantastic photos. Just one minute you are away from the busy downtown Toronto with a lovely boardwalk, tennis courts, picnic areas, an theme park, beaches, yacht club, restaurants and much more. Centre Island offers bike rentals for those who wish to cover plenty of ground in only a few hours; even tandem and quadricycles are available to tour the world of the Toronto Islands.

If you're planning to visit many of the major sites, it may make sense to buy a City Pass. It offers admission to the Royal Ontario Museum, CN Tower, Casa Loma, Hockey Hall of Fame, Ontario Science Centre, and Toronto Zoo. You have no reason to get bored when in Toronto. After seeing Toronto, your first thought may even be when to plan your next trip!

1) _____ Toronto is the capital city of Canada.

2) _____ Visitors in Toronto can feel Chinese culture.

3) _____ With over 4 000 event's annually, Harbourfront is the largest recreational spots in Canada.

4) _____ Visitors can do shopping in Eaton Center but can't find accommodation there.

5) _____ Center Island offers bike rentals for you to cover plenty of ground in only half an hour.

6) _____ With City Pass, you don't have to pay for your visit to Casa Loma in Toronto.

169

English for Tourism

Word Tips

gem:	珍品	prominent:	著名的
artifact:	工艺品	galleria:	游廊
auction:	拍卖	tandem:	两人前后座的自行车
boardwalk:	木板路		

2. Discuss: What makes Toronto so famous?

Toronto is a big, beautiful and efficient city which has emerged from relative obscurity over the past half century to become the center of culture, commerce and communications in Canada. Are you prepared for visiting Toronto?

Lead-in Questions:

1) Can you make a list of sightseeing attractions in Toronto?

2) What is the most prominent landmark in Toronto?

3) Can sports lovers enjoy themselves there? What can they do there?

4) What is the largest Canadian museum?

5) If you like shopping, where would you go in Toronto? Why?

Group Work: What makes Toronto so famous?

Step 1: Divide the class into groups.

Step 2: Ask students to discuss in details on sightseeing attractions in Toronto and the reasons why they would travel there.

Step 3: Have some groups give their presentations in front of the class.

Chapter 13　Travel Abroad 国外旅游

Singing for Travel 旅游歌曲

Breathless 无法呼吸

Shayne Ward

1. Singing English songs together with tourists can stimulate their interest, and liven up the atmosphere when they travel. Listen to the song casually with reference to the lyrics.

If our love was a fairy tale
I would charge in and rescue you
On a yacht baby we would sail
To an island where we'd say I do
And if we had babies they would look like you
It'd be so beautiful if that came true
You don't even know how very special you are
You leave me breathless

You're everything good in my life
You leave me breathless
I still can't believe that you're mine
You just walked out of one of my dreams
So beautiful you're leaving me breathless

And if our love was a story book

We would meet on the very first page
The last chapter would be about
How I'm thankful for the life we've made
And if we had babies they would have your eyes
I would fall deeper watching you give life
You don't even know how very special you are
You're everything good in my life
You leave me breathless
I still can't believe that you're mine
You just walked out of one of my dreams
So beautiful you're leaving me
You must have been sent from heaven to earth to change me
You're like an angel

The thing that I feel is stronger than love believe me
You're something special

English for Tourism

I only hope that I'll one day deserve what you've given me	So beautiful you're leaving me breathless
But all I can do is try	
Every day of my life	You're everything good in my life
You leave me breathless	You leave me breathless
	I still can't believe that you're mine
You're everything good in my life	You just walked out of one of my dreams
You leave me breathless	So beautiful you're leaving me
I still can't believe that you're mine	Breathless
You just walked out of one of my dreams	Breathless

2. One student role plays a tour guide while others act as tourists. Sing and enjoy the English song together.

Additional Know-how 知识扩展

Bus Tour in New York 纽约观光车

Without a doubt, New York Bus Tour is one of the best ways to see the major landmarks and attractions in New York, and to feel and take in the mood and spirit of the city. There are several companies in New York that organize and operate bus tours in the New York.

One of the major bus tour operators in New York is Gray Line New York Sightseeing that organizes bus tours in and around New York. The bus tours of the company cover all the major landmarks of New York City like Times Square,

Chapter 13 Travel Abroad 国外旅游

Central Park, Statue of Liberty and other attractions and landmarks of the city. The Gray Line New York Sightseeing organizes a variety of tours, such as Downtown Loop, Holiday Lights Tour, The Essential New York, NYC Showbiz Insiders Tour and many others. Each of these tours explores a particular aspect of the city.

One of the most popular bus tours of New York is the All Loops Tour. The bus tour comprises of a 48-hour double-decker bus tour that includes Uptown, Downtown, Brooklyn Loops and Night Tour. The All Loop Tour features 4 double Decker buses that will let you witness Manhattan and Brooklyn along with other attractions of New York, like Central Park, Lincoln Center, Times Square, Empire State Building, Brooklyn Museum, 5th & 7th Avenue boutiques, restaurants and shops and many other attractions.

If you do not have much time in your hand, the in-a-New-York-Minute Package is ideal for you. The tour comprises of Double Decker Downtown Loop, Ticket to The Empire State Building Observatory and Lady Liberty Harbor

English for Tourism

Cruise. The duration of the Downtown Loop is a little more than 2 hours and that of Lady of the Harbor Cruise is 45 minutes. The Downtown Loop will allow you to see sights of New York like Times Square, Empire State Building, Union Square shopping districts, Soho, Chinatown, Little Italy, Lower East Side, East Village, Rockefeller Center, Intrepid Sea-Air-Space Museum and more. Lady of the Harbor Cruise will take you to a 45 minutes trip around the Liberty Island that nestles the Statue of Liberty. The cruise will also let you enjoy mind boggling glimpses of Manhattan Skyline.

In any form of these bus tours, you can take advantage of sitting on top of the classic double-decker bus to enjoy an open-air tour of the enchanting city. Moreover, you can set the itinerary at your own pace. When you feel the need to hop off, do so at your whim. Hop on a Double Decker Bus when you feel you are ready to resume your intriguing tour.

Read the passage aloud, and decide whether the following statements are true or false. Write T for true and F for false.

1) _____ New York Bus Tour is the best way of seeing the city.

2) _____ The buses of New York Gray Line Sightseeing don't cover all the major landmarks in the city.

3) _____ If you are interested in seeing Manhattan and Brooklyn along with other attractions of New York in a double-decker, buses from All Loop Tour Company would be a good choice.

4) _____ Union Square is located in the Uptown area of New York City.

5) _____ You can get on and off the tour bus whenever you feel like it.

Chapter 14

Shopping
旅游购物

Focus on Learning 学习要点

- 旅游会话　　A Pair of Pants and A Pair of Shoes
　　　　　　　一条裤子、一双鞋
- 旅行故事　　Don't Have Any 什么也没有
- 旅游听力　　Old Fashioned Outlet Stores 老式工厂直销店
- 旅游视频　　Picking up Discount Clothing 挑选折扣价衣物
- 旅游阅读　　How did I shop at an Outlet?
　　　　　　　如何在工厂直销店里购物？
- 旅游写作　　A letter of sales proposal 销售意向书
- 旅游歌曲　　I Love you More than I can say 爱你在心口难开
- 知识扩展　　Outlet Shopping 工厂直销店购物

Useful Words and Expressions

coupon(优惠券)/ˈkuːpɔn/: a separate certificate or ticket entitling the holder to something as a gift or discount

outlet(直销店)/ˈautlet/: a shop that is one of many owned by a particular company and that sells the goods which the company has produced

offload(卸下)/ˈɔfləud/: get rid of something that you do not want by giving it to someone else

fraction(零头)/ˈfrækʃən/: a small part of something

retailer(零售商)/riːˈteilə/: a person or business that sells goods to public

inventory(存货)/ˈinvəntri/: the amount of goods a shop has or the value of them

shift(改变)/ʃift/: to move or change from one position or direction to another, esp. slightly

sample(样品)/ˈsæmpl/: a small amount of something which shows you what the rest is or should be like

second(次货)/ˈsekənd/: goods below the best in quality

turtleneck(高领衫)/ˈtəːtlneck/: (of a garment, esp a sweater) having a high, circular, close-fitting collar

chinos(丝光黄斜纹布裤)/tʃinəuˈskɔrədait/: cotton trousers, often of a pale color

alter(修改)/ˈɔːltə/: to change slightly

steel-toed army boots(钢钉军靴): durable boots that have a protective reinforcement in the toe

high-heels(高跟鞋)/hai ˈhiːltæp/: shoes to make people look taller

Chapter 14　Shopping 旅游购物

I. Dialogue

A Pair of Pants and A Pair of Shoes 一条裤子、一双鞋

1. Listen to the situational dialogue carefully, and match the information in column A with that in column B.

Column A	Column B
1) to express excitement over certain item	A. The waist is too big
2) to talk about the size of clothes	B. They are awesome
3) to alter the size of clothes	C. We take $5 for each alteration
4) to charge for extra service	D. They are 60% off
5) to talk about discount	E. The waist needs taking in

2. Listen to the situational dialogue again, repeat it sentence by sentence, and then role play it in pairs.

Mary:　Look at those leather pants! They are awesome!

Peter:　It must feel like a rock star! Should I try them on?

Mary:　Why not? The fitting room is over there.

Peter:　How do I look? They're really tight.

Mary:　Well, you're not ready for this kind of staff yet. Try these chinos.

177

English for Tourism

Peter: The waist is too big.

Mary: You can have it altered. Excuse me? Do you make alteration here? The waist needs taking in.

Staff: Yes, but we charge $5 for each alteration.

Mary: It's fine. We'll take this pair of pants. Can we pick it up later? We need to do some other shopping.

Staff: Sure.

Peter: Mary, look at this steel-toed army boots! They're pretty heavy but are very good for yard work. And they are 60% off !

Mary: Peter, you live in an apartment and work as a librarian. When can you wear it for your yard work?

Peter: Maybe someday, when I buy my own farm…

Mary: Then we can get your own steel-toed army boots. Excuse me? Do you have these red high-heels in size 8?

Peter: You never wear red shoes.

Mary: Who knows? Anyway, a girl can never have enough shoes.

II. Story—retelling

Listen to the funny story and retell it using your own words. You may refer to the key words or phrases given in the box.

| convenience | shrug | rumble | chopsticks |
| nope | mechanical | pencil | stomach |

Don't Have Any 什么也没有

A woman walks into a convenience store. She walks straight to the manager and asks, "Do you have any small notebooks?"

"Sorry," says the manager. "We're all out."

The woman shrugs, and asks, "Well, do you have any mechanical pencils?"

"Nope, don't have that either," says the manager.

Chapter 14 Shopping 旅游购物

The woman feels her stomach rumbling and asks, "Do you have plastic bags?"

The manager shrugs, "Sorry."

"Hmmph. How about chopsticks?" says the woman.

"Nope. Don't have that."

"Well," the woman says, "If you don't have anything, why don't you close the store?"

The manager shrugs, "Can't. Don't have the key."

Listening for Travel 旅游听力

Old Fashioned Outlet Stores 老式工厂直销店

1. Listen to the passage twice and fill in the blanks with the information you hear (one word for one blank).

When outlet stores first appeared, they were situated near their 1)_____ plant. That is how the 2)_____ came to be. It was an outlet for the manufacturer to sell its goods. They could cut out the 3)_____ man and by doing so they could offer their clothing at discount prices. These prices were very close to the actual 4)_____ price. The outlet stores would carry 5)_____ on orders they received. They would also have garments that had minor 6)_____ in them and therefore could not be sold in retail stores. The outlet stores didn't 7)_____ a lot of money primarily because they were not conveniently located to the public. The public didn't want to make

English for Tourism

a trip out of their way only to find out that the items they were looking for were 8)_____ or 9)_____. In a lot of cases the public had to rummage through bins of clothing to make a find. These were the real 10)_____ hunters.

2. Orally summarize the main ideas of the above passage and write them down on the following lines.

1) _____
2) _____
3) _____

Watching for Travel 旅游视频

Picking up Discount Clothing 挑选折扣价衣物

Brief information from the video:

Know where to shop, and where to get the best pieces for your money. You want to spend your money wisely, but you have to know the ins and outs. So, really look at it, even though it looks like a great deal, it is not the same quality as you could get.

The other thing that a lot of people don't consider is sales like last call at Neiman Marcus, Saks has something similar. A lot of these department stores have fabulous pieces that you can layer into your wardrobe.

Another option is going to consignment shops. It's another tricky thing because there are a lot of different types of consignment shops. You have to go

Chapter 14　Shopping 旅游购物

for the genre of the clothing that you like to wear.

One caution about that though. Watch out for the prices. In these consignment stores, sometimes, you would be ending up paying more for an older item. So just know it.

Also, get to know somebody at the stores that you like to shop in because they will clue you in about when the sales are going to happen and they will also pull items for you and hold them until they can ring them up and that's called pre-sell.

Watch the short video twice, and complete the following requirements.

Step 1: Divide the class into groups, and ask each student to take a note of what they have watched or heard. Compare the notes with their teammates.

Step 2: Make a brief summary of ways to pick up discount clothing according to the video.

Summary:

1) _____

2) _____

3) _____

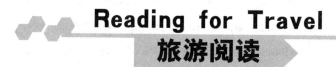

Reading for Travel 旅游阅读

How did I shop at an Outlet? 如何在工厂直销店里购物？

1. Listen to the passage and decide whether the following statements are true or false. Write T for true and F for false.

When I get to the outlet stores, I start by looking at the clearance racks. I generally beeline for the clearance sections. I try to combine clearance products with coupons or other offers if possible. If you aren't sure when you are going, check the outlet malls manufacturer's sites, they may have specific weekends which have bigger sales and promotions. I try not to be sidetracked by "deals", I come with a list of things I'm looking for, but I also don't get caught up in having to buy it, if there is no good deal, I go home without it.

The other thing I do is to shop with a buddy if I can. We have found that many of the promotions are so much off $100 or more, or $50 or more, but you only want to buy $25 worth. Well, if you go with someone else, we will have one person buy the lot and get the discount. We keep track in a notebook of who bought and owes what and try our best to keep it balanced throughout the day, at the end we work it out and even up. I've gotten a lot of good discounts this way.

I also don't let myself get into the name brand mindset. For me, the discount has to be good for any brand, not just because it has a fancy name brand. I might be willing to buy a fancy name brand shirt at about what I'd pay for a cheap full price shirt if the quality is significantly better, but I don't pay a ton more just because it has an expensive brand. So I rarely shop at all in the real high end clothing shops like Polo or Prada because even on sale and discounted, the clothing there is still too expensive for my preference.

Oh, don't forget to bring a calculator—sometimes the deals can be confusing to figure out how much you are really paying. One store at our trip last fall had a sale that went, Pants: 40% off, then 40% off everything in the store, then I had a coupon for 10% off one item. Much easier if you can just use a calculator.

  1) _____ When you are shopping at an outlet, the clearance section should be the first choice for bargain hunt.

  2) _____ You cannot use your coupons at the clearance products.

  3) _____ It's a good idea to go shopping with friends because you can get more discount this way.

Chapter 14　Shopping 旅游购物

4) _____ Those high-end clothing shops at outlets are at the same price ranges as those cheap clothes.

5) _____ The only value of outlet shopping lies in those big names brands.

6) _____ You'd know better how much discount you are given with the help of a calculator.

> **Word Tips**
> clearance products: 清仓产品　　　　full price: 全价
> beeline: 径直向某地走去　　　　mindset: 观念
> sidetrack: 把注意力转移到次要方面　name brand: 名牌

2. Discuss: How to make the most out of outlet shopping?

Outlets used to be bargain hunters' heaven, with all those quality merchandise at really low prices. But now, things are changing and prices at outlets are not always that rock-bottom low, and some merchandise there are not even worth the money and time. So discretion is important when one is shopping there. Work with your partner and discuss.

Lead-in Questions:

1) Have you or any of your friends got any experience in outlets shopping?

2) What are the reasons for shopping at outlets?

3) Do you think you can save a lot shopping at outlets, and why?

4) Do you often wear those clothes that you bought on sales at outlet stores?

5) Do you often regret about your bargain shopping? Why?

Group Work: How to make the most out of outlet shopping?

Step 1: Divide the class into groups.

Step 2: Ask students to discuss in details on the above questions and summarize the ways that can help you save a lot when you're shopping around. Give sufficient reasons.

Step 3: Have some groups give their presentations in front of the class.

English for Tourism

Writing for Travel 旅游写作

A letter of sales proposal 销售意向书

Read the following words and write a letter of sales proposal to promote an exhibition or an outlet in your city.

June 12, 2012

Dar-Hadassah Outlet Company

North Willington Avenue

West Palm Peach, Florida 33040

The United States

Dear Mr. Thompson:

Certainly enjoyed our telephone conversation on Thursday, and needless to say, we are gratified at the prospect of serving your company in August of 2008.

We could very comfortably accommodate you for arrival on Wednesday, August 18 with departure on Sunday, August 22, 2012. We could accept some early arrivals on Tuesday, August 17. However, it would be limited to 30 guest rooms. Therefore, the block of rooms we could make available to you looks something like this:

August, 2008

Day	Tuesday	Wednesday	Thursday	Friday	Saturday	Sunday
Date	17	18	19	20	21	22
Rooms	30	90	90	90	90	0

We have already established our convention rates for the calendar year 2012. Now, our Group Plan No.1 during August is RMB 700 Yuan single and RMB 1 000 Yuan double occupancy. Group Plan No.2 includes room, breakfast/lunch/dinner and is currently RMB 1 200 Yuan single and RMB 1 400 Yuan double occupancy. I've enclosed several descriptive brochures together with a most comprehensive fact sheet. As you can see, we do make available this area's most complete convention hotel. Please keep in mind that we are a five-star hotel.

If the arrangements I outlined are agreeable, please drop me a note and I shall reserve some space for you on a tentative basis so that the space does not disappear to another meeting planner.

Thank you again, and please let me know about your travel arrangements and your mobile phone so that I can set aide the necessary time to personally call you.

Cordially yours,

Zhang Xiaoyang

Sales Manager

Encl. Several descriptive brochures

Singing for Travel
旅游歌曲

I Love you More than I can say 爱你在心口难开
Leo Sayer

1. Singing English songs together with tourists can stimulate their interest, and liven up the atmosphere when they travel. Listen to the song casually with reference to the lyrics.

Whoa Whoa, yea yea

I love you more than I can say

I'll love you twice as much tomorrow

I love you more than I can say

Whoa Whoa, yea yea

I'll miss you every single day

Why must my life be filled with sorrow

I love you more than I can say

Oh don't you know I need you so

Oh tell me please I gotta know

Do you mean to make me cry

Am I just another guy

Whoa Whoa, yea yea

I miss you more than I can say

Why must my life be filled with sorrow

Oh love you more than I can say

Oh don't you know I need you so

Oh tell me please I gotta know

Do you mean to make me cry

Am I just another guy

Whoa Whoa, yea yea

I love you more than I can say

I'll love you twice as much tomorrow

Oh I love you more than I can say

I love you more than I can say

I love you more than I can say

2. One student role plays a tour guide while others act as tourists. Sing and enjoy the English song together.

Chapter 14　Shopping 旅游购物

Additional Know-how 知识扩展

Outlet Shopping 工厂直销店购物

Imagine shopping in a place where most items are 50% off every day of the week. As many bargain hunters know this is no dream, it's called a factory outlet.

What are factory outlets and what do they offer? Factory outlets are where big brands offload stock at a fraction of its normal value. In US, many states have outlet malls or factory outlets. Outlet centers, factory stores, and outlet malls all deal with major manufacturers trying to move stock. There are many reasons for this. For example, a retailer ships inven- tory to an outlet store because it isn't moving fast enough elsewhere or is general overstock. Companies also shift old stock to prepare for seasonal or industry changes. When retailers and manufacturers have gone out of business, they transfer inventory for resale at an outlet. Most outlets offer both normal stock and also samples and seconds. The stock is usually as good as new and retailers are required to inform you why an item is damaged. Usually, they can be products which have been slightly damaged or improperly made but are still good enough to be sold, just not at a prime retailer. Or, they are products never sold, perhaps for a reason, so rather than throwing them away, manufacturers breathe life into the products one more time through outlet sales.

With all considered, one expects to save a lot when shopping in outlets.

What kind of savings can one expect? Usually consumers can get 50%-70% off most major brands. For example, a pair of Sass & Bide jeans that costs $180 is available for $49 at an outlet while Gap white cotton turtleneck, which costs $16.50 for retail, is $3.99 here; Banana Republic women's Irish linen shirt, $88 retail, $29.99 here and many Baby Gap and Gap Kids items, up to $54 for retail, only cost $5 here.

While the merchandise seems like a steal with such good prices and reasons, one has to remember that the bottom line is that companies still want to make a profit, so not everything is going to be slashed to the rock bottom price all the time. There are still stages of sales cycles to go through, even when outlet shopping. So checking out what normal retail pricing is before hitting an outlet can help you decide if one item is a real windfall or not. Additionally, if the item isn't on your "usual" shopping list, the outlet price still may not be a bargain. If you normally wouldn't pay $600 for a designer bag, buying it for that price at an outlet center, even though it says with "50% off", doesn't make it a deal.

Read the passage aloud, and decide whether the following statements are true or false. Write T for true and F for false.

1) _____ You can always find discount items at an outlet.

2) _____ Retailers send their goods to an outlet because they sell well at other places.

3) _____ You can find the latest fashion at outlets centers with only a fraction of its normal price.

4) _____ Even though the goods are cheaper at outlets, all of them are products with flaws.

5) _____ Everything at an outlets is a real bargain.

Chapter 15

Emergencies
突发事件

Focus on Learning 学习要点

- 旅游会话　　A Car Accident 车祸事故
- 旅行故事　　Let's Make Sure He's Dead 确认他已死亡
- 旅游听力　　Emergency Medicines for Travel 旅游必备药品
- 旅游视频　　Security Tips for Travelers 旅游安全小知识
- 旅游阅读　　Knowledge about Emergency 应急知识
- 旅游歌曲　　Lemon Tree 柠檬树
- 知识扩展　　Travel Safety 旅游安全

Useful Words and Expressions

hazard(危险)/ˈhæzəd/: something causing unavoidable danger, peril, risk, or difficulty

seismic(地震的)/ˈsaɪzmɪk/: pertaining to, of the nature of, or caused by an earthquake or vibration of the earth, whether due to natural or artificial causes

endemic(地方的)/enˈdemɪk/: belonging exclusively or confined to a particular place

instability(不稳定)/ˌɪnstəˈbɪlɪti/: the quality or state of being unstable; lack of stability or firmness

inbound(归本国的)/ˈɪnbaund/: inward bound

prescription(处方)/prɪˈskrɪpʃən/: a direction, usually written, by the physician to the pharmacist for the preparation and use of a medicine or remedy

refill(替换物)/ˈriːˈfɪl/: a material, supply, or the like, to replace something that has been used up

laxative(通便的药)/ˈlæksətiv/: a medicine or agent for relieving constipation

diarrhea(腹泻)/ˌdaɪəˈriə/: an intestinal disorder characterized by abnormal frequency and fluidity of fecal evacuations

rehydration(补液)/ˌriːhaɪˈdreɪʃən/: the restoration of fluid to a dehydrated substance

dehydration(脱水)/ˌdiːhaɪˈdreɪʃən/: an abnormal loss of water from the body, esp. from illness or physical exertion

gauze(纱布)/gɔːz/: a surgical dressing of loosely woven cotton

Chapter 15　Emergencies 突发事件

I. Dialogue

A Car Accident 车祸事故

1. Listen to the situational dialogue carefully, and match the information in column A with that in column B.

Column A	Column B
1) person causing the car accident	A. insurance number and ID
2. damaged part of Sue's car	B. Jim
3. cause of the accident	C. the bumper
4. reason for Sue's saying to call the police	D. Jim's suddenly changing the lane without giving signals and overtaking Sue's car
5. items Jim shows to Sue	E. Jim denies it is his fault

2. Listen to the situational dialogue again, repeat it sentence by sentence, and then role play it in pairs.

Sue: Why did you run into me?

Jim: I didn't mean to. It was an accident.

Sue: You have completely damaged my car.

Jim: I did not. It looks perfectly fine.

English for Tourism

Sue: You don't see what happened to my bumper?

Jim: What did I do to it?

Sue: You smashed my bumper in with your car.

Jim: But this is not my fault.

Sue: You suddenly changed the lane without giving signals and tried to overtake me.

Jim: It is you who did the dangerous thing.

Sue: In this case, I'll call the police.

Jim: Stop doing it. Let me give you my car insurance number and show you my ID. I'll call to report this accident. My insurance company will take care of it shortly.

II. Story—retelling

Listen to the funny story and retell it using your own words. You may refer to the key words or phrases given in the box.

fall to the ground	roll back	cell phone	emergency services
operator	take it easy	make sure	a shot

Let's Make Sure He's Dead 确认他已死亡

A couple of hunters are out in the woods when one of them falls to the ground. He doesn't seem to be breathing; his eyes are rolled back in his head. The other hunter whips out his cell phone and calls the emergency services. He gasps to the operator, "My friend is dead! What can I do?" The operator, in a calm soothing voice, says, "Just take it easy. I can help. First, let's make sure he's dead." There is a silence, and then a shot is heard. The hunter's voice comes back on the line. He says, "OK, now what?"

Chapter 15   Emergencies 突发事件

Listening for Travel 旅游听力

Emergency Medicines for Travel 旅游必备药品

1. Listen to the passage twice and fill in the blanks with the information you hear (one word for one blank).

Nothing can ruin a vacation faster than an unexpected 1)_____ or injury. So before taking your next trip, be sure to 2)_____ a small kit of emergency supplies and medications in case the unexpected happens.

The most important items to remember to bring with you on any trip are an ample supply of your 3)_____ medications. With a good supply in hand, you won't have to worry about getting a 4)_____ if your luggage is lost or there's a 5)_____ in your returning flight.

6)_____ on how your body usually reacts when you're away from your home routines, you might want to bring along some antacids, a laxative, and/or anti-diarrheal medication. If you are traveling to an area where traveler's diarrhea is common, consider packing oral rehydration salts. Drinking these salts mixed with clean, bottled water can help offset dehydration 7)_____ by severe diarrhea.

Take along such 8)_____ emergency supplies as bandages, gauze and tape, eye drops, and antiseptic wipes. If you're embarking on a more active vacation, an elastic support bandage might come in handy for an unexpected strain or sprain.

Don't forget insect repellent and plenty of sunscreen. Though you probably won't use a vast 9)_____ of your emergency supplies during travel, chances are at least an item or two will turn out to be 10)_____. And that in itself makes it worth the space in your luggage.

193

2. Orally summarize the main ideas of the above passage and write them down on the following lines.

1) _____
2) _____
3) _____

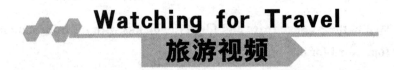

Watching for Travel 旅游视频

Security Tips for Travelers 旅游安全小知识

Brief information from the video:

Find out in terms of local area the US embassy. Because if you ever need anything, it is better to know where it is before you need it.

You need a copy of your passport. The reason you need that is because if someone takes your passport, you are not going to be able to identify yourself to the US embassy. You should leave one copy of this page at home; one copy with you and keep it somewhere else other than where your passport is.

Find out where the US embassy is before leaving the US. It will give you a list of the US embassy locations in all parts of the world. If the extra information you have to find out ahead of time and you don't need it, good for you, because that is the way you want it. But if you do need it, you are prepared. Make sure you are secure. And that starts with information.

Watch the short video twice, and complete the following requirements.

Step 1: Divide the class into groups, and ask each student to take a note of what they have watched or heard. Compare the notes with their teammates.

Chapter 15   Emergencies 突发事件

Step 2: Make a brief summary of advice given by the woman according to the video.

Summary:

1) _____

2) _____

3) _____

4) _____

5) _____

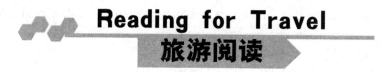

Knowledge about Emergency 应急知识

1. Survey: Take this fun quiz to test your knowledge about various disasters and emergency preparedness items.

1) As long as a thunderstorm is five miles away or farther from you, you are pretty safe from lightning strikes. This statement is (   ).

  A. True   B. False

2) When an earthquake strikes, you should (   ).

  A. Run outside to avoid falling building debris

  B. Take cover under a heavy piece of furniture

  C. Panic

  D. Lean against an inside wall or stand under an inside doorway

3) Which areas of the United States are vulnerable to earthquakes? (   )

  A. The West Coast, particularly California

B. The Eastern Seaboard

C. The central United States

D. All 50 states

4) What's the most common disaster that occurs in the United States? ( )

A. Fire   B. Flood

C. Earthquake   D. Tornado

5) What's the number one disaster related killer in the United States? ( )

A. Fire   B. Flood

C. Earthquake   D. Tornado

6) If your car stalls while you're evacuating from a flood, you should ( ).

A. Stay inside the car until assistance can arrive

B. Leave it

C. Call a towing service

D. Flag someone down to help you start it

7) When treating frostbite, you should ( ).

A. Rub the limbs down with snow

B. Give the victim a cup of hot chocolate to warm up

C. Gradually warm the body by wrapping in dry blankets

D. Plunge the affected areas in HOT water

8) The most dangerous part of a hurricane is ( ).

A. The breaking waves

B. The gale-force winds

C. The flood-causing rains

D. The landslides

Chapter 15　Emergencies 突发事件

Word Tips

lightning:	闪电	debris:	散落的碎片
vulnerable:	易受伤害的	tornado:	龙卷风
evacuate:	撤离	tow:	拖；拉
frostbite:	冻伤	plunge:	投入
hurricane:	飓风	gale-force:	强风的
landslide:	山崩		

2. Discuss: What items should be put in your travel emergency kit?

If you're planning an international trip, especially to a destination that's not a developed country, keeping a travel emergency kit can be a lifesaver.

Lead-in Questions:

1) Did you have any emergency during travelling?

2) How did you solve it with your prepared emergency kit?

3) Do you think it is necessary to have a travel emergency kit for international travel?

4) What factors should be taken into consideration when preparing a travel emergency kit?

Group Work: What items should be put in your travel emergency kit?

Step 1: Divide the class into groups.

Step 2: Ask students to discuss in details the above questions and summarize.

Step 3: Have some groups give their presentations in front of the class.

Singing for Travel
旅游歌曲

Lemon Tree 柠檬树
Fool's Garden

1. Singing English songs together with tourists can stimulate their interest, and liven up the atmosphere when they travel. Listen to the song casually with reference to the lyrics.

I'm sitting here in the boring room

It's just another rainy Sunday afternoon

I'm wasting my time, I got nothing to do

I'm hanging around, I'm waiting for you

But nothing ever happens, and I wonder

I'm driving around in my car

I'm driving too fast, I'm driving too far

I'd like to change my point of view

I feel so lonely, I'm waiting for you

But nothing ever happens, and I wonder.

I wonder how, I wonder why

Yesterday you told me about the blue-blue sky

And all that I can see is just the yellow lemon tree

I'm turning my head up and down

I'm turning, turning, turning, turning, turning around

And all that I can see is just another lemon tree.

I'm sitting here, I miss the power

I'd like to go out taking a shower

But there's a heavy cloud inside my head

I feel so tired, put myself into bed

Well nothing ever happens, and I wonder.

Isolation is not good for me

Isolation, I don't want to sit on a lemon tree

I'm stepping around in a desert of joy

May be anyhow I get another toy

And everything will happen, and you wonder.

I wonder how, I wonder why

Yesterday you told me about the blue-blue sky

And all that I can see is just another lemon tree

I'm turning my head up and down

Chapter 15　Emergencies 突发事件

I'm turning, turning, turning, turning, turning around	Yesterday you told me about the blue-blue sky
And all that I can see is just the yellow lemon tree.	And all that I can see
Yell I wonder wonder...	And all that I can see
I wonder how, I wonder why	And all that I can see is just the yellow lemon tree

2. One student role plays a tour guide while others act as tourists. Sing and enjoy the English song together.

Additional Know-how 知识扩展

Travel Safety 旅游安全

While most trips will be pleasant and without incident, it is a good idea to do some research and be prepared before you leave home. Be attentive to basic preparations (such as copying essential documentation and noting emergency contact information) and ensure that you are aware of any risk of seasonal natural hazards, seismic activity, extreme weather patterns, disease outbreaks or endemic health issues, personal security concerns, or any patterns of socio-political instability in your destination. One good place to start your research is with the websites of government agencies that report safety, security, and health issues related to travel in a foreign country.

Just as we travel to places with different climates and customs, we also travel to locations faced with different types of hazards that could interrupt our trip plans or have a potential impact on our health and security. Consequently, it

English for Tourism

is as important to familiarize ourselves with basic knowledge about cultural norms in a country as it is to be aware of any risks we may encounter while travelling. There are many sources that can prepare travelers for potential crisis event in a destination. Websites, such as news and weather sites and your country's foreign office website are good places to start.

If an event hits before you leave for your destination, there could be cancellation or postponement of inbound tourism. Check on the status of the event and if required, find out what the procedures may be place for altering your schedule.

Read the passage aloud, and decide whether the following statements are true or false. Write T for true and F for false.

1) _____ Basic preparations include copying essential documentation and noting emergency contact information.

2) _____ You should try to find out whether there are any patterns of socio-political instability in your destination.

3) _____ The website of government agencies is a good place to find information about safety, security, and health issues related to travel in a foreign country.

4) _____ We do not have to know basic knowledge about cultural norms in the destination country.

5) _____ If an event hits before you leave for your destination, you have to cancel your trip.

Chapter 16

Complaint Settlement
投诉处理

Focus on Learning 学习要点

- 旅游会话　　A Complaint about the Food　餐饮投诉
- 旅行故事　　I Don't Care　我无所谓
- 旅游听力　　To Whom Should I Complain?　我应当向谁投诉？
- 旅游视频　　A Complaint in the Restaurant　饭店投诉
- 旅游阅读　　Customer Service　客户服务
- 旅游写作　　A letter of complaints　投诉信
- 旅游歌曲　　Hey Jude　嘿，朱迪
- 知识扩展　　Make a Wise and Polite Complaint　有礼有节地投诉

Useful Words and Expressions

bother(烦扰)/ˈbɔðə/: to annoy, worry or cause problems for someone

assertive(确着无疑的)/əˈsəːtiv/: having or showing positive assurance

aggressive(好攻击的)/əˈgresiv/: quarrelsome, offensive

approach(处理)/əˈprəutʃ/: to deal with

defensive(防御的)/diˈfensiv/: quick to protect oneself from criticism

hostility(敌意)/hɔsˈtiliti/: enmity; ill will

Ranch Dressing(朗奇沙拉酱): a creamy buttermilk-based dressing with garlic and other spices and herbs

Thousand Island(千岛沙拉酱): a seasoned salad dressing made with mayonnaise, often containing chopped pickles, chili sauce, sweet peppers, hard-boiled eggs, etc.

compensation(补偿)/kɔmpenˈseiʃən/: something given or received as an equivalent for services, debt, loss, injury, suffering

Chapter 16　Complaint Settlement 投诉处理

Speaking for Travel 旅游会话

I. Dialogue

A Complaint about the Food 餐饮投诉

1. Listen to the situational dialogue carefully, and match the information in column A with that in column B.

Column A	Column B
1) complaint 1	A. no butter spreader
2) dressing ordered	B. overdone chicken
3) complaint 2	C. wrong salad dressing
4) complaint 3	D. Thousand Island
5) compensation	E. 50% off

2. Listen to the situational dialogue again, repeat it sentence by sentence, and then role play it in pairs.

Peter:　　Excuse me, Miss?

Waitress: Yes, sir. What can I do for you?

Peter:　　I'm afraid they have put the wrong dressing on my salad. This is Ranch Dressing, and I want Thousand Island.

Waitress: Oh, I'm awfully sorry. I'll get you another one.

Peter:　　Thank you. And can you bring me a butter spreader? I don't have

English for Tourism

one here. And my finger is not that clean.

Waitress: Sure! I'm so sorry, sir. Sometimes when we are in a hurry, we might make such mistakes. I'd be back with it right now.

Peter: Thanks! Listen, I really hate to bother you more, but my chicken is too tough. I tried but I really cannot take this.

Waitress: Oh, I'm terribly sorry, sir. I'll send it back to the kitchen. I can bring you something else, if you'd like.

Peter: Thank you. I think I'm done here. Can I have my bill?

Waitress: Sure, sir. We're so sorry about what happened. And we'll offer you a 50% discount as compensation. Hope to see you again.

Peter: Well, we'll see.

II. Story-retelling

Listen to the funny story and retell it using your own words. You may refer to the key words or phrases given in the box.

customer	bother	waiter
restaurant	air conditioner	turn up
turn down	surprisingly	angry

I Don't Care 我无所谓

A customer was bothering the waiter in a restaurant. First, he asked that the air conditioning be turned up because he was too hot. Then he asked it be turned down cause he was too cold, and so on for about half an hour.

Surprisingly, the waiter was very patient, he walked back and forth and never once got angry. So finally, a second customer asked him why he didn't throw out the pest.

"Oh I don't care." said the waiter with a smile. "We don't even have an air conditioner."

Chapter 16 Complaint Settlement 投诉处理

Listening for Travel 旅游听力

To Whom Should I Complain? 我应当向谁投诉？

1. Listen to the passage twice and fill in the blanks with the information you hear (one word for one blank).

When you'd like to 1)_____ a waiter in the restaurant, raise your hand, but don't wave. Most waiters are very busy but will get to you eventually. Be patient if the restaurant is 2)_____. The waiter might have many tables to help besides yours. Never yell or 3)_____ your fingers to get attention. Try to always remain polite. If your waiter is ignoring you, be patient, he or she may be busy and stressed out with too much work. Never 4)_____ out or stand up at your table looking for a waiter. It is rude. Don't ask your waiter's name just so you can shout it out across the room. Don't send out family members to look for the waiter especially children. It is dangerous in a busy restaurant.

When he does come to your table, talk to your waiter with respect. Control your tone and 5)_____, a bossy or 6)_____ way of speaking is not needed. Remember that if the food is cool or does not taste good that the waiter is not responsible. Avoid 7)_____ that will make your waiter want to pull out his or her hair and give you slow service. 8)_____ the waiter as "waiter," not "sir." If you cannot get any service, flag down another waiter or even a 9)_____. If you have 10)_____ service, complain to the restaurant manager, not to the waiter. It is more effective.

English for Tourism

2. Orally summarize the main ideas of the above passage and write them down on the following lines.

1) _____
2) _____
3) _____

Watching for Travel 旅游视频

A Complaint in the Restaurant 饭店投诉

Brief information from the video:

What you need: A substandard meal, a slow or rude waiter, a little righteous indignation and a sprinkling of tact.

Act immediately: Don't wait until you've eaten half of an inedible meal or for the bill to arrive to voice an objection.

Identify your aims: Think about what you hope to achieve by complaining.

What you expect: Make sure your suggested resolution matches your complaint.

Allergies and dislikes: It is worth telling the waiter of any allergies or aversions to particular ingredients while you're ordering.

Contain your rage: You are less likely to get what you want by being rude or aggressive with a waiter.

Be assertive: Don't be shy.

Polite behavior: If your concerns are not met with an acceptable resolution, ask politely to speak to the manager.

Tipping: If service has been poor, reducing the tip or not leaving one at all is acceptable. However, do remember to tip the waiter if he serves you well despite

Chapter 16　Complaint Settlement 投诉处理

the bad food.

Outside help: If after complaining to the waiter and the manager, you still feel like you have been fobbed off, it's time to take your complaints to a higher authority.

Illness: If once you've left a restaurant you become ill from food poisoning that can be traced back to the restaurant, you should report it to the food standards agency or department of health.

Compliment: As important as it is to complain if something has gone wrong during a meal, it's equally important to compliment and reward good or exceptional service.

Watch the short video twice, and complete the following requirements.

Step 1: Divide the class into groups, and ask each student to take a note of what they have watched or heard. Compare the notes with their teammate.

Step 2: Make a brief summary of ways to complain effectively in a restaurant according to the video.

Summary:

1) _____
2) _____
3) _____

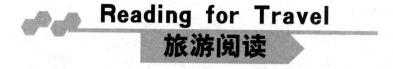

Customer Service 客户服务

1. Survey: Take this fun quiz to find out if you can offer good services to the customers.

1) You should greet and say the company's name when you answer the phone.

English for Tourism

☐ True ☐ False

2) Your clothes matter when dealing face to face with customers.

☐ True ☐ False

3) You should tell the customer if he/she is at fault.

☐ True ☐ False

4) Argue with the customer. Stand for your right.

☐ True ☐ False

5) Apologize to customer even if the fault was done by another staff.

☐ True ☐ False

6) When shaking hands, your hand should go soft and let the other party squeeze it.

☐ True ☐ False

7) Feedback by clients or customers is not important.

☐ True ☐ False

8) We must put ourselves in the customers' shoes if they lodge a complaint.

☐ True ☐ False

9) Repeat customer's complaint after they have said it to be sure.

☐ True ☐ False

10) Give away name cards with only one hand.

☐ True ☐ False

Word Tips

greet:	迎接	matter:	要紧
fault:	过错	apologize:	道歉
shake:	摇动	squeeze:	捏
feedback:	回馈	lodge:	正式提出

---

2. Discuss: Can you make a good service person?

As a service person, one might be dealing with 10 customers or 200 customers a day. Whether the interaction between you and your customer is a

Chapter 16 Complaint Settlement 投诉处理

positive or negative one largely depends on the way you react to their demand or complaint. Work with you partner and discuss:

Lead-in Questions:

1) Have you ever thought of working as a waiter or waitress? If not, why?

2) As a restaurant manager, how would you feel about people complaining a lot?

3) As a waiter or waitress, do you believe it is acceptable to stand up for one's right when the customer is unreasonable in his or her demands?

4) Do you think it is acceptable for a waiter or waitress to swear back if his or her customer swears first?

5) Do you believe the customer has the right to refuse to pay the bill if he is not happy with the service?

Group Work: Can you make a good service person?

Step 1: Divide the class into groups.

Step 2: Ask students to discuss in details on the above questions and summarize the characteristics a good service person should have.

Step 3: Have some groups give their presentations in front of the class.

Writing for Travel 旅游写作

A letter of complaints 投诉信

Read the following letter and write a letter of complaints in which you lodge a claim on the travel agency for the poor guiding service.

January 12, 2012

Jiujiang Overseas Travel Service, Ltd.
No. 17, 4th Block, 1st Ring Road,
Jiujiang, Jiangxi

Attn: Mr. Lin Yunzhi

Dear Mr. Lin,

We made a five-day trip around Jiujiang arranged by your travel service last month. We had a good time quite well for most of the time; however, we were dissatisfied with something unhappy which happened during our travel.

First, when we were in Jiujiang, the local guide took us to various curio and souvenir stores within our 2-day tour. It is true that we did want to buy some souvenirs to bring home; however, shopping for one or two times was enough because we came here for sightseeing after all. With too much time spent on shopping, our tour in the tourist sites was always in a hurry. It occurred often that we hardly arrived at the tourist sites when we had been asked to leave.

Second, according to the contract concluded between us we were to stay in a five-star hotel. However, we were transferred to a three-star hotel where the air-conditioner broke down during our stay. The heat of July in Jiujiang was nothing for the citizen there, but so unbearable for us that we couldn't fall asleep at night.

Therefore, we request you to give us an explanation and compensate us for 300 dollars per person due to your unreasonable arrangement.

We are looking forward to your prompt reply.

Sincerely yours,
Jane Moore

Chapter 16 Complaint Settlement 投诉处理

Singing for Travel
旅游歌曲

Hey Jude 嘿，朱迪

The Beatles

1. Singing English songs together with tourists can stimulate their interest, and liven up the atmosphere when they travel. Listen to the song casually with reference to the lyrics.

Hey Jude, don't make it bad
Take a sad song and make it better
Remember to let her into your heart
Then you can start to make it better
Hey Jude, don't be afraid

You were made to go out and get her
The minute you let her under your skin
Then you begin to make it better
And anytime you feel the pain, hey Jude, refrain
Don't carry the world upon your shoulders
For well you know that it's a fool who plays it cool
By making his world a little colder

Hey Jude, don't let me down

You have found her, now go and get her
Remember to let her into your heart
Then you can start to make it better
So let it out and let it in, hey Jude, begin
You're waiting for someone to perform with
And don't you know that it's just you, hey Jude, you'll do
The movement you need is on your shoulder

Hey Jude, don't make it bad
Take a sad song and make it better
Remember to let her under your skin,
Then you'll begin to make it
Better better better better better better, YEAH.

Na na na, na-na-na-na, na-na-na-na, hey Jude...

2. One student role plays a tour guide while others act as tourists. Sing and enjoy the English song together.

211

Additional Know-how
知识扩展

Make a Wise and Polite Complaint 有礼有节地投诉

When dining out, we hope everything will be perfect—nice surroundings, good food and good service. Sadly, that's not always the case. The wine may be wrong, the service might be disappointing, or something else goes wrong in the restaurant. When that happens, what can you do about it?

Most people may immediately choose to complain about what's bothering them and have their voice heard. This sometimes does not work out as we expect simply because the language we choose is not right. Remember no matter how unpleasant the situation, it's better to express your complaint politely. When complaining about your issue, you should be assertive, but not aggressive. If you approach the situation with angry words, people tend to react defensively, and you're more likely to be met with hostility instead of understanding. If you approach the situation with firmness in your position while keeping yourself calm and reasonable, you'll find people are less defensive and more ready to listen and willing to solve the issue. Starting a complaint with "I'm sorry to bother you" puts the listener who may have heard many complaints that day at ease. Use this phrase if the situation isn't that serious. For example, "I'm sorry to bother you, but I wanted whole wheat bread, not muffins." Everyone would much rather be asked to do something than told. Stating your complaint as a

Chapter 16 Complaint Settlement 投诉处理

request for help instead of a rebuke to the listener would be a shortcut to obtain what you want.

　　Besides speaking out how you feel, be prepared to listen. Just as you want to be heard, the person you are complaining to also has a right to be heard the same way you deserve. After you've made your position clear, step back and listen attentively to the response, even if you don't agree. It shows you to be fair and willing to work through the problem. If you approach the problem with due respect to people involved, it is more likely you will effectively be heard and have your problem solved.

Read the passage aloud, and decide whether the following statements are true or false. Write T for true and F for false.

1) _____ Only when you complain with strong language will they pay attention to your problem.

2) _____ People will be more cooperative if you complain in a polite and calm way.

3) _____ Besides being polite, it is also important to keep firm in your position.

4) _____ One fast way to solve your problem is to express your complaint as a request rather than a blame.

5) _____ When you are complaining, the service side has no right to speak how they feel.

Reference Keys 参考答案

Chapter 1　Reservation for Air Tickets 预订机票

Part One: Speaking for Travel 旅游会话

I. Dialogue

Flight Reconfirmation 航班再确认

1. Listen to the situational dialogue carefully and match the information in column A with that in column B.

1) C　　2) E　　3) D　　4) A　　5) B

2. Listen to the situational dialogue again, repeat it sentence by sentence, and then role play it in pairs. (omitted)

II. Story-retelling

I Know It's a Big Animal 我知道它是个大动物

Listen to the funny story and retell it using your own words. You may refer to the key words or phrases given in the box. (omitted)

Reference Keys 参考答案

Part Two: Listening for Travel 旅游听力

E- Ticket 电子机票

1. Listen to the passage twice and fill in the blanks with the information you hear (one word for one blank).

1) paperless   2) flight   3) hardcopy   4) assigned   5) departure
6) identification.   7) security   8) principal   9) expense   10) critical

2. Orally summarize the main ideas of the above passage and write them down on the following lines. (omitted)

Part Three: Watching for Travel 旅游视频

How to Save Money to Book Air Tickets? 如何省钱订机票?

Summary:

Consider Flying in Off-Peak Times

Flexibility is the key to an inexpensive getaway. If you say I'm going such and such a place and nowhere else on such and such a day, you limit your options. Discounts can be found during off-peak times and seasons. For example, everyone wants to see Europe during spring or summer. But, if you choose autumn or winter, you'll cut your costs big time.

Try Flying into Nearby Airports

Once you pick a city, consider flying into nearby airports. Instead of San Francisco, check prices for Oakland, San Jose, even Sacramento. Sometimes you can save a bundle arriving into one airport and leaving from another.

Be Flexible with Travel Dates

Research is essential to save your money. There are gobs of great online tools to help you find find the lowest fare. Some even send you alerts when prices drop between you favorite cities. Always direct these search engines to find fares for a few days before and after your dates, Twenty four hours can save you hundreds.

English for Tourism

Buy Direct from the Airline

Although these travel sites are great, they charge a service fee of at least $5 when it's time to book. So, I do my research with them and buy direct from the airline, where there's no fee and I sometimes get bonus miles for booking with them online. Don't even think about calling an airline to buy a ticket unless you absolutely have to. They all charge fees to talk with someone, in hopes you'll complete your purchase on the Internet.

Know When to Book Your Flight

The best time to book your tickets may be mid-week. Airlines usually announce fare sales around Wednesday or Thursday, and hike fares on the weekend. If you need to book at the last second, forget this and snag the best price you can find as soon as possible. You may want to site that let you name your own price, but sometimes they're the same price as the airlines themselves.

Sign Up for E-mail Alerts

Speaking of last minute tickets, you can find impressive bargains when booking just before take-off. The airlines offer e-mail blasts once a week letting you know how you can go on the cheap. As long as you don't get your heart set on a particular destination, you'll be on your way to frugal flying. And every penny you save getting there is one you can spend once you arrive. Thanks for watching.

Part Four: Reading for Travel 旅游阅读

Airline Reservations 机票预订

1. Listen to the passage and decide whether the following statements are true or false. Write T for true and F for false.

   1) F   2) F   3) T   4) F   5) T   6) F

2. Discuss: What are the advantages of booking air tickets online? (omitted)

Reference Keys 参考答案

Part Five: Singing for Travel 旅游歌曲

Country Road 乡村路带我回

John Denver

1. Singing English songs together with tourists can stimulate their interest, and liven up the atmosphere when they travel. Listen to the song casually with reference to the lyrics. (omitted)

2. One student role plays a tour guide while others act as tourists. Sing and enjoy the English song together. (omitted)

Part Six: Additional Know-how 知识扩展

Travel Agency 旅行社

Read the passage aloud, and decide whether the following statements are true or false. Write T for true and F for false.

1) F   2) T   3) F   4) T   5) T

Chapter 2　Airport Check-in 机场登机

Part One: Speaking for Travel 旅游会话

I. Dialogue:

Weight Limit 行李限重

1. Listen to the situational dialogue carefully, and match the information in column A with that in column B.

1) D   2) E   3) B   4) C   5) A

2. Listen to the situational dialogue again, repeat it sentence by sentence, and then role play it in pairs. (omitted)

English for Tourism

II. Story-retelling:

Kissing the Luggage Goodbye 与行李吻别

Listen to the funny story and retell it using the key words or phrases given in the box. (omitted)

Part Two: Listening for Travel 旅游听力

Online Check-in 网上检票

1. Listen to the passage twice and fill in the blanks with the information you hear (one word for one blank).

1) confirm   2) boarding   3) specific   4) preferred   5) promoted

6) check-in   7) available   8) scheduled   9) benefits   10) request

2. Orally summarize the main ideas of the above passage and write them down on the following lines. (omitted)

Part Three: Watching for Travel 旅游视频

How to Get to the Airport on Time? 如何按时到达机场？

Summary:

Catching a flight is tricky. Leave too early and you'll sit at the gate for hours; leave too late and you might miss your plane. You'll need a computer or phone, a car, car service or bus schedule and radio.

Step 1: confirm your departure time the morning of or the night before your flight, either by calling your airline or checking online.

Step 2: visit the Transportation Security Administration's website at www.tsa.gov for security waiting times at all the major airports. Sign up for updates from your airline's website, which will call or email you alerts if there are any changes in your itinerary.

Step 3: listen to the radio traffic report for accidents and construction projects that might slow you down. Budget your time accordingly.

Step 4: if you're leaving your car at the airport, visit the airport's website to find out exactly where long- and short-term parking is located. Also, map the best route online. Research the best way to get from the parking lot to the main terminal.

Step 5: if you're getting a ride with a service or even a friend, confirm when and where the driver is picking you up. If you're taking the bus, double-check the schedule.

Step 6: if you're taking a cab, leave plenty of time to catch one—especially in the rain.

Step 7: if you're headed to a big airport, call on your way to confirm that your departure gate and check-in terminal hasn't changed.

Step 8: when you arrive, have your ticket and I.D. out. It will help get you through check-in faster.

Part Four: Reading for Travel 旅游阅读

Expressions Related to Air Travel 航空旅游相关表述

1. Survey: Take this quiz to find out how much you know about expressions related to air travel. Words in the following box are for your reference.

1) passport	2) domestic	3) international	4) flight number
5) customs	6) ticket	7) check in	8) flight
9) claim check	10) reservation	11) seat assignment	12) window seat
13) aisle seat	14) baggage	15) baggage claim	16) visa
17) boarding pass	18) gate	19) carry on	

2. Discuss: What do you need to do before and after arriving at the airport? (omitted)

English for Tourism

Part Five: Writing for Travel 旅游写作

Customs Declaration Form 海关申报表

Fill in the a Customs Declaration Form and present it to the Customs officials. Make a dialogue between the tourist and the Customs officials. (omitted)

Part Six: Singing for Travel 旅游歌曲

Big Big World 大千世界

Emilia

1. Singing English songs together with tourists can stimulate their interest, and liven up the atmosphere when they travel. Listen to the song casually with reference to the lyrics. (omitted)

2. One student role plays a tour guide while others act as tourists. Sing and enjoy the English song together. (omitted)

Part Seven: Additional Know-how 知识扩展

ABC about Airport Check-in 机场登机常识

Read the passage aloud, and decide whether the following statements are true or false. Write T for true and F for false.

1) T   2) F   3) T   4) F   5) F

Chapter 3   On the Flight 飞行途中

Part One: Speaking for Travel 旅游会话

I. Dialogue:

In-flight TV Programs and Channels 机上电视节目和频道

1. Listen to the situational dialogue carefully and match the information in

column A with that in column B.

1) D   2) C   3) E   4) A   5) B

2. Listen to the situational dialogue again, repeat it sentence by sentence, and then role play it in pairs. (omitted)

II. Story-retelling:

The Plane is Crashing into the Ocean 飞机要掉到海里啦

Listen to the funny story and retell it using the key words or phrases given in the box. (omitted)

Part Two: Listening for Travel 旅游听力

Useful Tips Onboard 机上有用小贴士

1. Listen to the passage twice and fill in the blanks with the information you hear (one word for one blank).

1) instructions   2) location   3) Safety   4) unsure   5) respectful
6) illegal   7) board   8) right   9) Inform   10) exercises

2. Orally summarize the main ideas of the above passage and write them down on the following lines. (omitted)

Part Three: Watching for Travel 旅游视频

How to Recover from Jet Lag? 怎样倒时差？

Summary:

There are a few things you could do that I want to share with you today that will help you out in your quest to avoid the doldrums of jet lag. First of all, did you know that it can be avoided almost entirely by drinking a lot of water. I mean almost entirely, stay hydrated during your flight. Jet lag, not a good thing and recovering to new time zones means you have to do a couple of things. Set your watch the moment you get on the plane for your new destination. In other words, if it gets six hours in advance, go ahead and set that so that you can mentally adjust on your watch. Another thing, stay hydrated. As I mentioned, if you stay hydrated, you're going to be having a much better chance of retaining nutrients in your body as well as vitamins and minerals. Those planes are really areas that will dehydrate the body. Therefore, avoid alcoholic beverages and caffeine. Avoid salty snacks like nuts and I'm going to suggest that you try to sleep as much as possible on the plane, depending on the time you arrive in your new destination. Eat vitamins and stay healthy and you'll overcome that jet lag within a few days.

Part Four: Reading for Travel 旅游阅读

Are Blind Pilots Flying? 盲人飞行员在飞吗?

1. Listen to the passage and decide whether the following statements are true or false. Write T for true and F for false.

1) F   2) T   3) T   4) T
5) F   6) F   7) F   8) T

2. Discuss: What kind of image a trustworthy pilot should have? (omitted)

Part Five: Singing for Travel 旅游歌曲

Take Me To Your Heart 将我带入你的心

Michael Learns To Rock

1. Singing English songs together with tourists can stimulate their interest, and liven up the atmosphere when they travel. Listen to the song casually with reference to the lyrics. (omitted)

2. One student role plays a tour guide while others act as tourists. Sing and enjoy the English song together. (omitted)

Reference Keys 参考答案

Part Six: Additional Know-how 知识扩展

In-flight Services 机上服务

Read the passage aloud, and decide whether the following statements are true or false. Write T for true and F for false.

1) T   2) F   3) F   4) F   5) T

Chapter 4 Landing at the Airport 抵达机场

Part One: Speaking for Travel 旅游会话

I. Dialogue:

Proper Way to Fill out the Forms 正确的填表方法

1. Listen to the situational dialogue carefully, and match the information in column A with that in column B.

1) C   2) A   3) B   4) D   5) E

2. Listen to the situational dialogue again，repeat it sentence by sentence, and then role play it in pairs. (omitted)

II. Story-retelling:

We're Still on the Ground 我们还在地上

Listen to the funny story and retell it using the key words or phrases given in the box. (omitted)

Part Two: Listening for Travel 旅游听力

Landing Announcement 飞机降落机场通知

1. Listen to the passage twice and fill in the blanks with the information you hear (one word for one blank).

1) aircraft   2) complete   3) seatbelts   4) remain   5) sign
6) smoke   7) overhead   8) flight   9) injure   10) forward

223

English for Tourism

2. Orally summarize the main ideas of the above passage and write them down on the following lines. (omitted)

Part Three: Watching for Travel 旅游视频

United Airlines Touched Down at San Francisco
联合航空公司航班抵达旧金山

Summary:

Before landing, you should prepare to clear the US immigration, claim their luggage, and clear the US customs.

The following passenger's service program is brought to you by United Airlines.

Please join us as we welcome you to the United States and to San Francisco, California. The spirit of warm San Francisco springs from the city's cultural and commercial diversity. Welcome to San Francisco, golden city by the bay.

We will be landing at the San Francisco international airport. The airport is located 16 miles, 25.7 kilometers, south of the downtown San Francisco. The airport has a north and south terminal, a central terminal and an international terminal. Most united international flights arrive at concourse G of the international terminal.

Because this is an international flight, all passengers must clear US immigration, claim their baggage and clear US customs in San Francisco.

Have your passport and completed travel documents ready for the immigration officer.

Upon entering immigration you will be directed to the appropriate lane, please have your passport and completed travel documents ready for the immigration officer. Every arriving passenger must complete the US custom declaration form in English in full. If the family is travelling together, the head of the household must complete the form. Only one form per family is required.

All food and agricultural products must be declared on the US customs declaration form.

Reference Keys 参考答案

If you have a visitor's visa, you'll need to complete the white immigration form; if you do not have a visitor's visa and travelling under the visa waiver program, use the green form.

All forms must be completed in blue or black ink and write only in capital letters. It is important to accurately complete both the arrival and departure records on these forms. If you are completing the green form, you must also complete the back, be sure to sign the date on the back of the green form.

If you need help completing the forms, please ask your flight attendant or United Airlines representative for assistance. Detailed instructions for completing these forms can be found in the back of your hemisphere magazine. Remember customs and immigration forms must be completed in full before presenting them to the immigration officer.

After clearing the immigration, proceed to the baggage claim area to reclaim your baggage.

All passengers including those connecting to another flight must claim their baggage. Electronic signs will identify the baggage carousel assigned to your flight. For your convenience, courtesy baggage carts are available. After collecting your baggage, proceed to US customs and agriculture, if you are not sure whether an item can or cannot be brought into the US, declare it or ask a US customs or an agriculture inspector for assistance. Have your completed US costumes form ready for the inspector.

Passengers with connecting domestic flights will recheck their baggage.

Passengers with connecting domestic flights will recheck their baggage in the baggage recheck area outside the customs. Look for flight information monitors for your departure gate. Your airline representative will also provide you with your connecting flight departure terminal and gate assignment. Make sure your baggage is checked though to your final destination. United Airline's domestic flights operate from the north terminal, concourse F. It's an easy walk from the international terminal to united tickets counters and gates located in concourse F. A free shuttle bus service is also provided between airport terminals to assist travelers making airline connections.

More Information about United Airline

If San Francisco is your final destination, you'll exit customs to the airport arrival's hall. Currency exchange, car rental services, hotel directories and taxi, ground transportation services are available as you leave.

United Airlines is a founding member of the Star Alliance, the world's leading airline alliance. Information of our alliance partners and our co-sharing relationship with other leading airlines can be found in your hemispheres magazine.

Again, welcome to San Francisco. If this is your final destination we wish your stay is enjoyable.

Part Four: Reading for Travel 旅游阅读

Instructions on the Declaration Form 报关表须知

1. Listen to the passage and decide whether the following statements are true or false. Write T for true and F for false.

1) F   2) F   3) T   4) T   5) F   6) T

2. Discuss: How to deal with the Declaration Form? (omitted)

Part Five: Writing for Travel 旅游写作

Arrival Card 入境登记卡

Fill in an Arrival Card and present it to the immigrant officials in the airport. Make a dialogue between the tourist and immigrant officials. (omitted)

Part Six: Singing for Travel 旅游歌曲

Right Here Waiting 此情可待

Richard Marx

1. Singing English songs together with tourists can stimulate their interest, and liven up the atmosphere when they travel. Listen to the song casually with reference to the lyrics. (omitted)

2. One student role plays a tour guide while others act as tourists. Sing and enjoy the English song together. (omitted)

Part Seven: Additional Know-how 知识扩展

1) F   2) T   3) T   4) F   5) T

Chapter 5　Tourism Transportation 旅游交通

Part One: Speaking for Travel 旅游会话

I. Dialogue:

Travel by Taxi 搭乘出租车

1. Listen to the situational dialogue carefully, and match the information in column A with that in column B.

1) D   2) C   3) A   4) B   5) E

2. Listen to the situational dialogue again, repeat it sentence by sentence, and then role play it in pairs. (omitted)

II. Story-retelling:

The Train Has Broken Down 火车开不动了

Listen to the funny story and retell it using the key words or phrases given in the box. (omitted)

Part Two: Listening for Travel 旅游听力

Travel by Train in the USA 美国火车旅游

1. Listen to the passage twice and fill in the blanks with the information you hear (one word for one blank).

1) operate   2) scenery   3) routes   4) young   5) atmosphere
6) spreading   7) mountains 8) crossing 9) deserts 10) telegraph

English for Tourism

2. Orally summarize the main ideas of the above passage and write them down on the following lines. (omitted)

Part Three: Watching for Travel 旅游视频

Cabs in New York City 纽约出租车

Summary:

There's more to taking a taxi in New York City than hailing it down. You've got to know how to survive the ride.

You Will Need

I. Attentiveness.

II. Some street savvy.

III. Money for the fare.

IV. Knowledge of your rights.

Step 1: Know where you're going

Before you hail a cab, get a rough idea of how far you're going and how much it should cost. If you're not sure, ask a New Yorker. Most will be happy to help you avoid getting ripped off by an unscrupulous cabbie.

Step 2: Step off the curb

Step off the curb and face the oncoming traffic. Just don't step so far off the curb that you're standing in a lane of traffic.

Step 3: Hail a cab

Hail a cab by raising your arm when you spot one with its middle roof light on, indicating it's available. If no lights are on, it's occupied. If the outer lights are on, it's off duty. If it's a livery car or limo—and not a real yellow cab—it's not supposed to stop, so don't get in.

Step 4: Avoid busy areas

Don't try to hail a cab just slightly in front of someone else with their arm out—it's rude. If you're in an area where lots of people are trying to get cabs, walk a few blocks to a less competitive location. New York cabs go off duty around 4:00 in the afternoon to change shifts, which makes finding a free one almost impossible. Try hailing an off-duty cab by indicating with your fingers that you're only going a short distance—if the cabbie is going your way anyway, he might just take you.

Step 5: Enter and exit on sidewalk

Play it safe by always getting in—and out—of the cab on the same side as the sidewalk. Only four passengers are allowed in a regular-sized taxi—unless the fifth passenger is under 7 and seated on someone's lap.

Step 6: Know your rights

You have the right to tell the driver which route to take, you can ask him to slow down, and you are in control of the heat, AC, and radio. You are also entitled to be driven anywhere in the five boroughs. If the driver says he doesn't go outside Manhattan, politely contradict him and make a note of his medallion number—located on the window shield dividing the front seat from the rear—so you can report him if need be.

Step 7: Buckle up

Better safe than sorry.

Step 8: Watch the meter

When you hop in the cab, the fare starts at $2.50. The meter will increase 40 cents every fifth of a mile (approximately four blocks) or, if you're standing still or crawling along slowly, once every minute. There is no extra charge for luggage. On weekdays from 4 p.m. to 8 p.m., there's an extra $1 surcharge. And every night after 8 p.m., there is a night surcharge of 50 cents.

Step 9: Know airport fares

Know your airport fares. La Guardia is a regular metered fare, but you're also responsible for any tolls along the way. If you're going from JFK to Manhattan, or vice versa, there's a flat fare of $45 plus tolls. If you're heading to Newark airport, there is an extra $15 charge plus return tolls to New York City. Note that New York City cabs can drop you at Newark airport, but because it's out of state, they're not legally allowed to pick up fares.

Step 10: Pay the fare

Pay the fare, and unless you had the worst ride of your life, add a nice tip:

cab drivers work hard for the money. 10 to 20 percent tip is customary.

Step 11: Get a receipt

Always get the receipt. It has the taxi's medallion number on it, which will come in handy if you accidentally leave something in the cab. And before you get out, take a last look around, inside and out.

Part Four: Reading for Travel 旅游阅读

Interesting Things about Transport 交通工具趣闻

1. Survey: Take this fun quiz to find out some facts about transport.

1) C   2) A   3) C   4) B   5) B
6) A   7) A   8) A   9) B   10) C

2. Discuss: What's your preference, public transportation or private car? (omitted)

Part Five: Singing for Travel 旅游歌曲

Scarborough Fair 斯卡堡集市
Sarah Brightman

1. Singing English songs together with tourists can stimulate their interest, and liven up the atmosphere when they travel. Listen to the song casually with reference to the lyrics. (omitted)

2. One student role plays a tour guide while others act as tourists. Sing and enjoy the English song together. (omitted)

Part Six: Additional Know-how 知识扩展

Read the passage aloud, and decide whether the following statements are true or false. Write T for true and F for false.

1) F   2) T   3) F   4) T   5) F

Chapter 6 Hotel Check-in 入住酒店

Part One: Speaking for Travel 旅游会话

I. Dialogue:

Changing Reservation 改订房间

1. Listen to the situational dialogue carefully, and match the information in column A with that in column B.

1) C   2) A   3) B   4) E   5) D

2. Listen to the situational dialogue again, repeat it sentence by sentence, and then role play it in pairs. (omitted)

II. Story-retelling:

Don't Treat Us like We're a Couple of Fools 别把我们当成一对傻瓜

Listen to the funny story and retell it using the key words or phrases given in the box. (omitted)

Part Two: Listening for Travel 旅游听力

Tips for Hotel Reservation 酒店预订技巧

1. Listen to the passage twice and fill in the blanks with the information you hear (one word for one blank).

1) reservation   2) restrictions   3) entail   4) return   5) deal
6) budget   7) expenses   8) lodges   9) competing   10) Peak-season

2. Orally summarize the main ideas of the above passage and write them down on the following lines. (omitted)

English for Tourism

Part Three: Watching for Travel 旅游视频

Hotel and Front Desk Clerk 酒店和度假村前台人员

Summary:

1) The front desk clerk is usually the first person a guest encounters when checking into a hotel or motel.

2) In addition to performing the specific duties, the desk clerk has the responsibility of making a great first impression. It is important to be able to quickly and efficiently follow the steps needed to get the guest check in.

3) Being knowledgeable about the checking-out times, hotel services and local attractions is essential. But personal warmth, friendliness, and good interpersonal skills are more important.

4) When travelers reach their hotel, they are often tired or stressed. The desk clerk's job is to make them feel truly welcomed and comfortable. So they will make a point of staying at your hotel every time when they are in town.

5) The front desk is an excellent place to start if you are interested in career of hotel management since it allows you to learn about the many different aspects involving in running a hotel efficiently and places you on the front line of customer relations.

Part Four: Reading for Travel 旅游阅读

Documents for Hotel Check-in 酒店入住文件

1. Listen to the passage and decide whether the following statements are true or false. Write T for true and F for false.

1) T   2) T   3) F   4) F   5) T   6) T

2. Discuss: What documents do you need for hotel check-in? (omitted)

Part Five: Writing for Travel 旅游写作

Laundry Registration 衣物清洗表

Fill in a Laundry Registration and present it to the maid. Make a situational dialogue accordingly. (omitted)

Part Six: Singing for Travel 旅游歌曲

Sunny Came Home 阳光走进家门
Shawn Colvin

1. Singing English songs together with tourists can stimulate their interest, and liven up the atmosphere when they travel. Listen to the song casually with reference to the lyrics. (omitted)

2. One student role plays a tour guide while others act as tourists. Sing and enjoy the English song together. (omitted)

Part Seven: Additional Know-how 知识扩展

Front Desk/Reservation Desk 前台

Read the passage aloud, and decide whether the following statements are true or false. Write T for true and F for false.

1) F   2) T   3) F   4) T   5) F

Chapter 7　Hotel Check-out 退房结账

Part One: Speaking for Travel 旅游会话

I. Dialogue:

A Late Check-out 延时退房

1. Listen to the situational dialogue carefully, and match the information in

column A with that in column B.

    1) C   2) E   3) B   4) A   5) D

2. Listen to the situational dialogue again, repeat it sentence by sentence, and then role play it in pairs. (omitted)

II. Story-retelling:

The Hotel Bill 饭店账单

Listen to the funny story and retell it using the key words or phrases given in the box. (omitted)

Part Two: Listening for Travel 旅游听力

How to Save Money on Hotel Bills? 怎样节省酒店开支？

1. Listen to the passage twice and fill in the blanks with the information you hear (one word for one blank).

    1) typically   2) bills   3) cheaper   4) specials   5) qualify

    6) letterhead   7) guarantees   8) official   9) available   10) affordable

2. Orally summarize the main ideas of the above passage and write them down on the following lines. (omitted)

Part Three: Watching for Travel 旅游视频

A Checklist for Check-out 退房结账清单

Summary:

Traveling is one of my favorite things to do in the whole world. And while coming home after a big trip can be as comforting as a big fuzzy blanket, it's a real pain to discover anything you've somehow left behind. But take a look at this hotel checkout checklist, and you won't be smacking yourself in the forehead when you get back. Check it out.

Tip 1: take your time packing before you check out. Allowing yourself a few extra minutes to calmly get everything back into your suitcase will reduce your chances of carelessly forgetting anything. If you're pressed for time, you can always call the front desk and request a late checkout, which will often buy you another hour. And really, until they start calling to pester you about leaving and threatening to charge you another night unless you get out immediately, you've got nothing to worry about.

Tip 2: do a complete sweep of the room. Once everything obvious is in your bags, be sure to check all the nooks and crannies: drawers, the night stand, closets, the safe, under the bathroom sink, under the bed, and if you've got one, the refrigerator. As you're about to leave the room, do one final pass over the entire area——and be sure to check under the covers, too. That's pretty much where I usually find all my socks and boxers.

Tip 3: leave a tip. It's best to tip your housekeeper on a nightly basis, so that the person who does the actual tidying up is the one who gets the tip. But either way, leave cash in the amount of three to five bucks per night at a fancy hotel, and one or two at a less fancy joint, and be sure to leave it in a properly marked envelope.

And finally, when you're actually checking out, be sure to review your entire bill. Check that all of the charges are exact, and make sure you have a paper statement or receipt to walk away with. Remember that now is the time to dispute anything funky——the second you walk out the door it gets a little bit tougher.

Part Four: Reading for Travel 旅游阅读

Avoid Extra Hidden Fees 避免额外的隐性费用

1. Listen to the passage and decide whether the following statements are true or false. Write T for true and F for false.

1) T   2) T   3) F   4) T   5) T   6) F

2. Discuss: If you are charged unreasonably, what will you do? (omitted)

English for Tourism

Part Five: Singing for Travel 旅游歌曲

I still believe 我仍然相信
Mariah Carey

1. Singing English songs together with tourists can stimulate their interest, and liven up the atmosphere when they travel. Listen to the song casually with reference to the lyrics. (omitted)

2. One student role plays a tour guide while others act as tourists. Sing and enjoy the English song together. (omitted)

Part Six: Additional Know-how 知识扩展

ABC for Hotel Check-out 退房结账常识

Read the passage aloud, and decide whether the following statements are true or false. Write T for true and F for false.

1) T   2) F   3) F   4) T   5) T

Chapter 8   Theme Parks 主题公园

Part One: Speaking for Travel 旅游会话

I. Dialogue:

Disneyland Theme Park 迪斯尼主题公园

1. Listen to the situational dialogue carefully, and match the information in column A with that in column B.

1) B   2) A   3) C   4) E   5) D

2. Listen to the situational dialogue again, repeat it sentence by sentence, and then role play it in pairs. (omitted)

Reference Keys 参考答案

II. Story-retelling:

Roller Coaster 过山车

Listen to the funny story and retell it using the key words or phrases given in the box. (omitted)

Part Two: Listening for Travel 旅游听力

Tips for Saving Tickets to Theme Parks 主题公园门票省钱窍门

1. Listen to the passage twice and fill in the blanks with the information you hear (one word for one blank).

1) coupons   2) corporate   3) benefits   4) deals   5) charge

6) teenagers   7) sunburn   8) multi-day   9) regional   10) locals

2. Orally summarize the main ideas of the above passage and write them down on the following lines. (omitted)

Part Three: Watching for Travel 旅游视频

A Travel to Universal Studio of Hollywood
好莱坞环球电影制片公司之旅

Summary:

My favorite part of Universal Studios of Hollywood is the studio tour. It's my chance to show you real Hollywood movie making on the world famous backlot. Come to see devastation beyond imagination, created for the site of World War II; meet the giant life-like character from King Kong and experience the explosive hard driving action of The Fast and the Furious, extremely close up; plus you get to visit the sites of award-winning TV shows. Ready to be part of today's working Hollywood? Check it out!

English for Tourism

Part Four: Reading for Travel 旅游阅读

A Brief Introduction of the Disneyland 迪斯尼主题公园简介

1. Listen to the passage and decide whether the following statements are true or false. Write T for true and F for false.

1) F 2) F 3) T 4) F 5) T 6) F

2. Discuss: How much do you know about Disneyland? (omitted)

Part Five: Writing for Travel 旅游写作

Commentary 导游词

Cruising on the Huangpu River 巡游黄浦江

Read the commentary and write a commentary of a tourist site that you know and make a presentation in your class. Pay attention to your body language. (omitted)

Part Six: Singing for Travel 旅游歌曲

Hotel California 加州旅馆

The Eagles

1. Singing English songs together with tourists can stimulate their interest, and liven up the atmosphere when they travel. Listen to the song casually with reference to the lyrics. (omitted)

2. One student role plays a tour guide while others act as tourists. Sing and enjoy the English song together. (omitted)

Reference Keys 参考答案

Part Seven: Additional Know-how 知识扩展

A Money-and-Time Effective Way to Visit Theme Parks
省钱省时玩转主题公园

Read the passage aloud, and decide whether the following statements are true or false. Write T for true and F for false.

1) T   2) T   3) F   4) F   5) F

Chapter 9   Get-togethers 聚会派对

Part One: Speaking for Travel 旅游会话

I. Dialogue:

A Cocktail Party 鸡尾酒会

1. Listen to the situational dialogue carefully, and match the information in column A with that in column B.

1) C   2) D   3) A   4) E   5) B

2. Listen to the situational dialogue again, repeat it sentence by sentence, and then role play it in pairs. (omitted)

II. Story-retelling:

Free Advice at Social Affairs 社交聚会上的免费建议

Listen to the funny story and retell it using the key words or phrases given in the box. (omitted)

Part Two: Listening for Travel 旅游听力

A Bonfire Party 篝火晚会

1. Listen to the passage twice and fill in the blanks with the information you hear (one word for one blank).

1) occur   2) company   3) closest   4) secretive   5) beach

6) second   7) spot   8) supplies   9) adjusting   10) memorable

2. Orally summarize the main ideas of the above passage and write them down on the following lines. (omitted)

Part Three: Watching for Travel 旅游视频

How to Deal with Unexpected Guests? 如何应对不速之客？

Summary:

Step 1: Be polite. As the perfect host, your first priority is to accommodate the surprise arrival. They probably didn't know they weren't invited, and when they realize the inconvenience of their presence they will probably feel very embarrassed. Put them at their ease, welcome them into your home and offer them a drink.

Step 2: Squeeze them in. While they are busy talking to the other guests, disappear into the dinning room and squeeze another place onto the table set up. It might disrupt your otherwise perfect arrangements, but at this point you don't have many options, short of kicking them out. And that would be like shooting a puppy.

Step 3: Split the portions. If dinner is a serve yourself affair, then the extra guest is easy to accommodate—simply adjust the portions accordingly. However, if you have prepared six portions of chicken—not seven—then you have no alternative but to split delightful niece Tara's portion with her surprise partner. Politely excuse this when serving up. "I'm terribly sorry, I only cooked for six, but I know Tara won't mind sharing."

Step 4: Speak to offender afterwards. When dealt with in a polite and dignified manner, your surprise guest should pose little problem once dinner is under way. Relax and enjoy the evening. Either in private or after the event you are perfectly entitled to make your delightful niece realize that her actions were completely unacceptable.

Part Four: Reading for Travel 旅游阅读

How to throw a surprise party? 如何举办惊喜聚会?

1. Listen to the passage and decide whether the following statements are true or false. Write T for true and F for false.

1) T   2) F   3) T   4) T
5) F   6) T   7) T   8) F

2. Discuss: If you are to throw a surprise party, what will you do? (omitted)

Part Five: Singing for Travel 旅游歌曲

Only Time 唯有时光

Enya

1. Singing English songs together with tourists can stimulate their interest, and liven up the atmosphere when they travel. Listen to the song casually with reference to the lyrics. (omitted)

2. One student role plays a tour guide while others act as tourists. Sing and enjoy the English song together. (omitted)

Part Six: Additional Know-how 知识扩展

A Successful Party 成功的派对

Read the passage aloud, and decide whether the following statements are true or false. Write T for true and F for false.

1) F   2) T   3) T   4) T   5) F

English for Tourism

Chapter 10　Foods and Drinks 餐饮酒水

Part One: Speaking for Travel 旅游会话

I. Dialogue:

Taking an Order for Western Food 点西餐

1. Listen to the situational dialogue carefully, and match the information in column A with that in column B.

1) B　　2) D　　3) A　　4) C　　5) E

2. Listen to the situational dialogue again, repeat it sentence by sentence, and then role play it in pairs. (omitted)

II. Story-retelling:

Pardon Me, Ma'am 对不起，夫人

Listen to the funny story and retell it using the key words or phrases given in the box. (omitted)

Part Two: Listening for Travel 旅游听力

Table Etiquette 餐桌礼仪

1. Listen to the passage twice and fill in the blanks with the information you hear (one word for one blank).

1) remove　2) lap　3) inappropriate　4) wipe　5) plate
6) leave　7) glass　8) farthest　9) utensil　10) dessert

2. Orally summarize the main ideas of the above passage and write them down on the following lines. (omitted)

Part Three: Watching for Travel 旅游视频

Etiquette for Ordering Wine 点葡萄酒的礼仪

Summary:
Do not be afraid of asking waiter for advice.

Hi, I am Brendan Walsh and today we are discovering the wonderful world of wine. In this clip, I am going to discuss the proper etiquette for ordering wine in a restaurant. The primary purpose of ordering wine in restaurant is to ensure that you get a suitable pairing between your entree and the wine. Do not be afraid to ask the waiter or sommelier for advice. Just let them know the entree that you are having as well as your price range and they should be able to recommend a good selection.

Verify the wine is in fact what you order.

Once you agreed on a selection, the waiter will bring the wine out to you and present it in a manner such as this. As the host, it's your responsibility to verify that that is in fact the wine that you order not just the name of the wine, but also the vintage. The same wine can be different prices depending on the vintage.

After the waiter uncorks the wine, don't smell the cork. Look at the cork and deduce whether or not the cork is tented.

Once the waiter shows you the wine and you agree that this is the wine you in fact selected. They will go ahead and uncork the wine and he shoots up the cork on the table. Now, don't go and smell the cork as it's not going to give you any value, it is just going to smell like cork, but what you can do is to look at the cork and deduce whether or not, the cork is tinted or the wine maybe tinted based on cork discoloration. For example, I can see that the cork itself is a nice tan color and within the cork at the mouth of it, it s a deep red. That tells me two things, number one, the wine has been stored properly on its side, so that the wine rested against the cork which help prevent oxidation. And number two, because it is tan and there is no discoloration here I know or I think I know that the wine is not spoiled or oxidized. So, it will just give you clues in to what to expect from the wine.

After the waiter pours a small amount, the host should swirl, sniff and taste the wine to ensure it is not spoiled.

Now, as the host the waiter is going to go ahead and pour a small amount of wine into your glass, your job as the host is to swirl, sniff the wine, and taste the wine, this is my favorite part. This is not an opportunity for you to send back a perfectly good bottle of wine that you just don't care for. The point of tasting the wine is just to ensure that it is not spoiled or it's corked. Once you tell the waiter that yes you accept the wine, the waiter will go clock wise around the table to your party and fill each person's glass, ladies first. As the host, your glass will be topped off last.

Next, I am going to talk about primary differences between red and white wine.

Part Four: Reading for Travel 旅游阅读

Idioms Relating to Foods and Drinks 餐饮酒水相关成语

1. Survey: Take this fun quiz to find out a number of common expressions which are derived from food and drink items.

1) B   2) C   3) B   4) A   5) C   6) D

2. Discuss: What are similarities and differences between food in American culture and Chinese culture? (omitted)

Part Five: Writing for Travel 旅游写作

Notice 通知

Read the notice about account settlement in the hotel. Make a dialogue between the guest and the cashier. (omitted)

Part Six: Singing for Travel 旅游歌曲

Say you, Say me 说你，说我

Lionel Richie

1. Singing English songs together with tourists can stimulate their interest, and liven up the atmosphere when they travel. Listen to the song casually with reference to the lyrics. (omitted)

2. One student role plays a tour guide while others act as tourists. Sing and enjoy the English song together. (omitted)

Part Seven: Additional Know-how 知识扩展

American Food 美国菜

Read the passage aloud, and decide whether the following statements are true or false. Write T for true and F for false.

1) F   2) T   3) F   4) T   5) T

Chapter 11　Footing the Bill 付账买单

Part One: Speaking for Travel 旅游会话

I. Dialogue:

A Miscalculated Bill 账单出错

1. Listen to the situational dialogue carefully, and match the information in column A with that in column B.

1) C   2) D   3) E   4) B   5) A

2. Listen to the situational dialogue again，repeat it sentence by sentence, and then role play it in pairs. (omitted)

II. Story-retelling:

The Bill 账单

Listen to the funny story and retell it using the key words or phrases given in the box. (omitted)

English for Tourism

Part Two: Listening for Travel 旅游听力

ABC about Tipping in the USA 美国小费常识

1. Listen to the passage twice and fill in the blanks with the information you hear (one word for one blank).

1) situations   2) charge   3) expected   4) practice   5) equal
6) 10%   7) tipping   8) general   9) range   10) type

2. Orally summarize the main ideas of the above passage and write them down on the following lines. (omitted)

Part Three: Watching for Travel 旅游视频

How to Tip in a Restaurant? 怎样在饭店付小费?

Summary:

Tipping is the easy way to reward a waiter who helps you to have an enjoyable meal. But rules vary depending on the situation and level of service. Followings are simple guide for easy tipping and minimum embarrassment.

Step 1: you will need some cash or a credit card and a generous spirit.

Step 2: Evaluating Service. When deciding how much you should leave for a tip, think about your overall enjoyment of the meal and how or if the waiting staff has contributed to it.

Step 3: The average tip. 10% of the final bill is a nominal amount you should tip, and is expected if the staff have delivered normal, adequate service. This may vary depending on the quality of service and is a sliding scale from 0% to 25%.

Step 4: When to give a big tip. There are several occasions when leaving a larger tip than 10% is appropriate and could be anything up to 40%. If the service is unusually helpful, friendly and unobtrusive, if your waiter has been particularly knowledgeable about the food and wine, if your waiter has gone out of their way to accommodate an unusual request or problem, or if you are a large group of six or over.

Step 5: When to leave a small tip. If the waiter has done less than the bare minimum and has been generally unhelpful, it is appropriate that your tip should reflect that. Also if the waiter gets the order wrong or doesn't pay attention to special requirements and food allergies, then you are within your rights to reduce the tip. In the rare occasion that a waiter is actually rude or abusive to a customer, the tip should be dramatically reduced or removed. However be careful that you are not penalizing the wrong person for problems during your meal. If the chef cooked something badly but your waiter handled the situation well by apologizing immediately and replacing the dish, then they still deserve a good tip.

Step 6: When to leave no tip at all. No tipping at all sends a strong message about the level of service you have received. Reserve 0% tips for venues to which you never wish to return as you may find it difficult to get a table once you've made known your disappointment.

Step 7: Included discretionary tip. Increasingly restaurants are choosing to include a discretionary or optional charge with the final bill which can vary from about 12% to 15%. While an optional charge takes away the hassle of having to work out a tip, remember it is just that-optional. If the service doesn't live up to their suggested tip, then don't be embarrassed to remove it.

Step 8: Tipping by card. In some restaurants you will be given the option to leave a tip on your credit card when paying the bill. This is a simple and discreet way of tipping but bear in mind that the restaurant may use that tip as a contribution to its waiting staff's wages. To ensure that the waiter actually receives all of the tip, it may be best to leave it for them in cash.

Step 9: Tipping in cash. Once you have paid the bill, leave the desired amount on the table in a neat pile. If there is a tray or a bill wallet left on the table, you can leave it on or in them. Never thrust money into the waiter's hand during the meal or as you leave as it could potentially be embarrassing for the waiter. If you don't have the correct change for a tip, don't be embarrassed about asking your waiter to break a note.

English for Tourism

Step 10: In a hurry. If you are in a hurry and are paying for your bill and service in cash, it is acceptable to pay the waiter for the meal with enough excess to cover his tip and immediately leave.

Part Four: Reading for Travel 旅游阅读

The Bills on Who? 谁来付钱

1. Listen to the passage and decide whether the following statements are true or false. Write T for true and F for false.

1) T   2) F   3) T   4) F
5) T   6) T   7) F   8) T

2. Discuss: If your friends ask you to dine out in a restaurant, who do you think should pay the bill? (omitted)

Part Five: Singing for Travel 旅游歌曲

Let It Be 由它去

The Beatles

1. Singing English songs together with tourists can stimulate their interest, and liven up the atmosphere when they travel. Listen to the song casually with reference to the lyrics. (omitted)

2. One student role plays a tour guide while others act as tourists. Sing and enjoy the English song together. (omitted)

Part Six: Additional Know-how 知识扩展

Tips for Paying the Bill 结账小窍门

Read the passage aloud, and decide whether the following statements are true or false. Write T for true and F for false.

1) T   2) F   3) T   4) F   5) T

Reference Keys 参考答案

Chapter 12　Cruise Travel 邮轮旅游

Part One: Speaking for Travel 旅游会话

I. Dialogue:

Ready for Getting Aboard the Ship 准备登船

1. Listen to the situational dialogue carefully, and match the information in column A with that in column B.

1) B　　2) D　　3) A　　4) E　　5) C

2. Listen to the situational dialogue again, repeat it sentence by sentence, and then role play it in pairs. (omitted)

II. Story-retelling:

God Could Not Save Me 上帝救不了我

Listen to the funny story and retell it using the key words or phrases given in the box. (omitted)

Part Two: Listening for Travel 旅游听力

The Cabins of a Liner 邮轮舱位

1. Listen to the passage twice and fill in the blanks with the information you hear (one word for one blank).

1) based　　2) cabin　　3) expensive　　4) located　　5) spacious

6) luxurious　　7) distinctions　　8) alike　　9) occur　　10) debarking

2. Orally summarize the main ideas of the above passage and write them down on the following lines. (omitted)

Part Three: Watching for Travel 旅游视频

How to Cut Down the Costs for Cruise Travel?

如何减少邮轮旅行开支？

Summary:

A cruise is a wonderful, relaxing way to vacation. It can be affordable, too, if you know the right places to cut costs.

You Will Need:

- Research
- A travel agent
- Adequate planning time
- Empty plastic bottles
- Booze
- Transportation

Optional:

- Stocks (optional)
- A soda sticker (optional)

Step 1: Research and hire travel agent

Research cruise lines to find those that go to your destination. Hire a travel agent who specializes in those lines. Be sure to ask about discounts offered by that line.

Step 2: Buy early and buy cruise-only

Buy early, in the off-season, and buy a cruise-only package without airfare. Book your own flights and transfers because air-inclusive packages cost more.

Step 3: Book a small cabin

Book a small cabin without a view to save money. There are so many activities on the ship that you will hardly use your room.

Step 4: Be a VIP

Ask your travel agent to tell the cruise line that you are a VIP and that you intend to be a frequent customer. You might be rewarded with a free upgrade.

You can purchase an on-board soda sticker for a set price and then enjoy unlimited quantities of soda while on your cruise.

Step 5: BYOB

Bring your own alcohol on the cruise and you will save lots of money. Fill plastic bottles with liquor and then use your unlimited soda sticker for mixers. Bring wine and pay only a corkage fee at dinner.

Step 6: Secure your own ground transport and tours

Secure your own ground transportation when in port, as well as your own private land tours. These measures will cost much less than cruise buses and tours.

Step 7: Watch out for cash-guzzling extras

Limit your purchase of cash-guzzling extras, such as shipboard photos, bar purchases, and onboard art auctions.

Step 8: Purchase next cruise

Purchase your next cruise while on your cruise. You will get a better deal on the package as well as more credits to use on the ship.

Do you know: the Queen Mary, now harbored in Long Beach, California, had a 31-year career as a luxury cruise liner and World War II troop carrier?

Part Four: Reading for Travel 旅游阅读

Water Excursions at Cancun 坎昆水上旅游

1. Listen to the passage and decide whether the following statements are true or false. Write T for true and F for false.

1). F   2) T   3) F   4) T   5) T   6) F

2. Discuss: Can we take Cancun and develop our tourism in certain areas, and how? (omitted)

English for Tourism

Part Five: Writing for Travel 旅游写作

Tour Itineraries 旅游线路

Read the following tour itinerary and arrange a 5-day itinerary for a group in your city, and discuss it with the tour leader. (omitted)

Part Six: Singing for Travel 旅游歌曲

Upside down 颠倒

A-Teens

1. Singing English songs together with tourists can stimulate their interest, and liven up the atmosphere when they travel. Listen to the song casually with reference to the lyrics. (omitted)

2. One student role plays a tour guide while others act as tourists. Sing and enjoy the English song together. (omitted)

Part Seven: Additional Know-how 知识扩展

1) T   2) F   3) F   4) F   5) T

Chapter 13   Travel Abroad 国外旅游

Part One: Speaking for Travel 旅游会话

I. Dialogue:

Walking in the Wall Street   漫步华尔街

1. Listen to the situational dialogue carefully, and match the information in column A with that in column B.

1) D   2) E   3) A   4) C   5) B

2. Listen to the situational dialogue again, repeat it sentence by sentence, and then role play it in pairs. (omitted)

II. Story-retelling:

The Same Good Fortune 同样好运

Listen to the funny story and retell it using the key words or phrases given in the box. (omitted)

Part Two: Listening for Travel 旅游听力

An Unforgettable Trip to Niagara Falls 尼亚加拉瀑布难忘之旅

1. Listen to the passage twice and fill in the blanks with the information you hear (one word for one blank).

1) jet   2) views   3) highlights   4) mighty

5) total   6) personal   7) cruise   8) soaked

2. Orally summarize the main ideas of the above passage and write them down on the following lines. (omitted)

Part Three: Watching for Travel 旅游视频

Travel Guide——Ottawa 旅游指南：渥太华

Summary:

Ottawa, is Canada's fourth largest city. And today we'll continue our travel series with a look at Canada's capital. Located in the Ottawa Valley, Ottawa is the capital of Canada and it was chosen as such by Queen Victoria in 1857 for its strategic location as a compromise between the two colonies and their French and English population.

The climate of Ottawa has a very extreme range of temperature, with the record high being 100 degrees Fahrenheit. The city receives roughly 93 inches of snow annually between middle December and early April. Day time temperature in January averages 13 degrees Fahrenheit. Average temperature in July is 80 degrees Fahrenheit. It attracts roughly 3 million visitors each year. Ottawa's Parliament Hill is home to Canada's landmark of the Parliament Buildings. The best known of the Parliament Building is the Centre Block which includes the Peace Tower in national symbol. Inside the Centre Block are the House of Commerce and the Senate of Chambers and the Library of Parliament. The entire Parliament to compound measures 112 360 square miles.

The Rideau Canal connects Ottawa on the Ottawa River to Kinston on Lake Ontario. Registered as a UNESCO World Heritage Site in 2007, the canal measures 126 miles long. Today boat tourism on the canal is offered and recreational boaters use it to travel between Ottawa and Kinston.

Showcase in over 300 000 tulips, Ottawa plants more of the flowers for capital than any of the other city. Tulip bulbs were given from the Dutch royal family in 1945 after Canada sheltered the Princess during the Word War II and played a large part in the libration of the Netherlands.

Ottawa's Canadian Museum of Civilization is Canada's most visited museum tracing over a thousand years in Canadian history. The National Gallery of Canada holds the world's most comprehensive collection of Canadian and Indian arts.

Ottawa is also the home to the world's largest collection of huge mazes, with Saunders Farms housing 9 large mazes and a series of puzzle mazes.

With over 50 galleries, theaters in this area, heritage buildings, parks and shopping locations, the toughest problem for visitors in Ottawa is to decide what to do.

Part Four: Reading for Travel 旅游阅读

Discover Toronto 多伦多发现之旅

1. Listen to the passage and decide whether the following statements are true or false. Write T for true and F for false.

1) F   2) T   3) F   4) F   5) F   6) T

2. Discuss: What makes Toronto so famous? (omitted)

Part Five: Singing for Travel 旅游歌曲

Breathless 无法呼吸
Shayne Ward

1. Singing English songs together with tourists can stimulate their interest, and liven up the atmosphere when they travel. Listen to the song casually with reference to the lyrics. (omitted)

2. One student role plays a tour guide while others act as tourists. Sing and enjoy the English song together. (omitted)

Part Six: Additional Know-how 知识扩展

Bus Tour in New York 纽约观光车

Read the passage aloud, and decide whether the following statements are true or false. Write T for true and F for false.

1) F   2) F   3) T   4) F   5) T

Chapter 14　Shopping 旅游购物

Part One: Speaking for Travel 旅游会话

I. Dialogue:

A Pair of Pants and A Pair of Shoes 一条裤子、一双鞋

1. Listen to the situational dialogue carefully, and match the information in column A with that in column B.

1) B   2) A   3) E   4) C   5) D

2. Listen to the situational dialogue again，repeat it sentence by sentence, and then role play it in pairs. (omitted)

English for Tourism

II. Story-retelling:

Don't Have Any 什么也没有

Listen to the funny story and retell it using the key words or phrases given in the box. (omitted)

Part Two: Listening for Travel 旅游听力

Old-fashioned Outlet Stores 老式工厂直销店

1. Listen to the passage twice and fill in the blanks with the information you hear (one word for one blank).

1) manufacturing   2) name   3) middle   4) wholesale   5) overruns

6) flaws   7) generate   8) damaged   9) unavailable   10) bargain

2. Orally summarize the main ideas of the above passage and write them down on the following lines. (omitted)

Part Three: Watching for Travel 旅游视频

Picking up Discounted Clothing 挑选折扣价衣物

Summary:

The next thing is to do a little homework. Know where to shop, and where to get the best pieces for your money. You want to spend your money wisely, but you have to know the ins and outs. A lot of people believe in going to outlets to shop, which is great, because you can definitely find great things there. But you have to be careful because a lot of outlets stores get things made especially for them which are sort of a lesser quality than you would find in a department store. So, really look at it, even though it looks like a great deal, it is not the same quality as you could get, for instance, in a Banana Republic store, or something sometimes they make especial things for Banana outlets. So keep that in mind.

The other thing that a lot of people don't consider is sales like last call at

Neiman Marcus, Saks has something similar. A lot of these department stores have fabulous pieces that you can layer into your wardrobe. They would be totally attention-getting. You don't want to spend a huge amount on them, but by the time they are in the last call, they are marked down three or four times and then they're 50% off of that, so you are really getting a great piece for a total fraction of the cost.

Another option, of course, my favorite option since I own one consignment boutique, is going to consignment shops. It's another tricky thing because there are a lot of different types of consignment shops. Some are specializing on clothing, uhh, you know, you have to go for the genre of the clothing that you like to wear, uhh, our store specializes more on contemporary looks. We go for one of kilt things, the effect of season was very big on dresses, but there are other consignment shops that were more conservative, which, if it's your thing, great!

One caution about that though. Watch out for the prices. Because, again, in these consignment stores, sometimes the prices there are a lot higher for something that's one or two years old, than it would be if you went and got something at last call at Nieman's or a Saks thing. You would be ending up paying more for an older item. So just know it.

Also, get to know somebody at the stores that you like to shop in because they will clue you in about when the sales are going to happen and they will also pull items for you and hold them until they can ring them up and that's called pre-sell. So keep all that in mind before you go.

Part Four: Reading for Travel 旅游阅读

How did I Shop at an Outlet? 如何在工厂直销店里购物？

1. Listen to the passage and decide whether the following statements are true or false. Write T for true and F for false.

1) T   2) F   3) T   4) F   5) F   6) T

2. Discuss: How to make the most out of outlet shopping? (omitted)

257

Part Five: Writing for Travel 旅游写作

A letter of sales proposal 销售意向书

Read the following words and write a letter of sales proposal to promote an exhibition or an outlet in your city. (omitted)

Part Six: Singing for Travel 旅游歌曲

I Love you More than I can say 爱你在心口难开
Leo Sayer

1. Singing English songs together with tourists can stimulate their interest, and liven up the atmosphere when they travel. Listen to the song casually with reference to the lyrics. (omitted)

2. One student role plays a tour guide while others act as tourists. Sing and enjoy the English song together. (omitted)

Part Seven: Additional Know-how 知识扩展

Outlet Shopping 工厂直销店购物

Read the passage aloud, and decide whether the following statements are true or false. Write T for true and F for false.

1) T   2) F   3) F   4) F   5) F

Chapter 15   Emergencies 突发事件

Part One: Speaking for Travel 旅游会话

I. Dialogue:

A Car Accident 车祸事故

1. Listen to the situational dialogue carefully, and match the information in

column A with that in column B.

    1) B   2) C   3) D   4) E   5) A

2. Listen to the situational dialogue again, repeat it sentence by sentence, and then role play it in pairs. (omitted)

II. Story-retelling:

Let's Make Sure He's Dead 确认他已死亡

Listen to the funny story and retell it using the key words or phrases given in the box. (omitted)

Part Two: Listening for Travel 旅游听力

Emergency Medicines for Travel 旅游必备药品

1. Listen to the passage twice and fill in the blanks with the information you hear (one word for one blank).

1) illness   2) pack   3) prescription   4) refill   5) delay

6) Depending   7) caused   8) essential   9) majority   10) helpful

2. Orally summarize the main ideas of the above passage and write them down on the following lines. (omitted)

Part Three: Watching for Travel 旅游视频

Security Tips for Travelers 旅游安全小知识

Summary:

Find out in terms of local area the US embassy.

We are going to talk about security. When you travel in other parts of the world, it is very important, especially if you are going to be in a very new area, southeast Asia, Polynesia for the first time or Europe for that matter, find out in terms of the local area US embassy, because if you ever need anything, it is better to know where it is before you need it.

You need a copy of your passport.

Now one of the ways that can help you when you are travelling to find the local US embassy is you need a copy of your passport, this page specifically. The reason you need that is because if someone takes your passport, you are not going to be able to identify yourself to the US embassy. You should leave one copy of this page at home; take one copy with you and keep it somewhere else other than where your passport is.

Find out where the US embassy is before you leave the US.

Now where do you go to find out where the local US embassy is? You need to find out before you leave the US. It will give you a list of the US embassy locations in all parts of the world. You know right where you have to go. Even if you are going to several different countries, this is a matter of your personal security. If the extra information you have to find out ahead of time and you don't need it, good for you, because that is the way you want it. But if you do need it, you are prepared. Make sure you are secure. And that starts with information.

Part Four: Reading for Travel 旅游阅读

Knowledge about Emergency 应急知识

1. Survey: Take this fun quiz to test your knowledge about various disasters and emergency preparedness items.

1) B. If you can hear thunder, you could be in danger. Just because the storm is not right on top of you, does not mean that you are safe. Lightning can strike as much as 10 miles away from the rainy area. Be sure to take cover in a building or car, if possible. However, you can estimate how far the storm is from you. Just count the seconds between when you see the lightning flash and hear the thunder crack, and divide by five.

2) Either B or D. Take cover under something heavy, like a sturdy desk or chair. Or you can use an inside wall or doorway. Just make sure to keep away from where glass could shatter, like mirrors or windows.

3) D. Even though earthquakes occur most frequently west of the Rocky Mountains, all 50 states and US territories are at risk for an earthquake.

Forty-one of those states and territories are at moderate to high risk for earthquakes to strike.

4) A. More homes will be threatened by fire than by any other disaster. This is one of the reasons why a fire escape plan is crucial for every home. Flood is the second most common disaster.

5) B. Floods, particularly flash floods, are the number one weather and disaster related killer in the US. Flash floods cause an average death toll close to 150 people a year.

6) B. Leave your car and move to higher ground. Many deaths have occurred when people try to move their stalled cars in a flood.

7) C. Make sure the victim has dry clothes, and wrap him/her in a blanket. The body temperature needs to rise gradually, to avoid damage. Do NOT give them hot drinks or any drink with caffeine. As a stimulant, caffeine can speed up the heart, and quicken the effect that cold has on the body.

8) A. Even though much death and destruction is caused by wind, rain, and landslides, it is the breaking waves, known as the storm surge that causes the most damage. During a hurricane, this wall of water slams into the coastline, causing flash floods and structural damage to buildings.

2. Discuss: What's your idea of travel and romance? (omitted)

Part Five: Singing for Travel 旅游歌曲

Lemon Tree 柠檬树

Fools Garden

1. Singing English songs together with tourists can stimulate their interest, and liven up the atmosphere when they travel. Listen to the song casually with reference to the lyrics. (omitted)

2. One student role plays a tour guide while others act as tourists. Sing and enjoy the English song together. (omitted)

English for Tourism

Part Six: Additional Know-how 知识扩展

Travel Safety 旅游安全

Read the passage aloud, and decide whether the following statements are true or false. Write T for true and F for false. (omitted)

1) T   2) T   3) T   4) F   5) F

Chapter 16　Complaint Settlement 投诉处理

Part One: Speaking for Travel 旅游会话

I. Dialogue:

A Complaint about the Food 餐饮投诉

1. Listen to the situational dialogue carefully, and match the information in column A with that in column B.

1) C   2) D   3) A   4) B   5) E

2. Listen to the situational dialogue again，repeat it sentence by sentence, and then role play it in pairs. (omitted)

II. Story-retelling:

I Don't Care 我无所谓

Listen to the funny story and retell it using the key words or phrases given in the box. (omitted)

Part Two: Listening for Travel 旅游听力

To Whom Should I Complain? 我应当向谁投诉？

1. Listen to the passage twice and fill in the blanks with the information you hear (one word for one blank).

1) summon   2) packed   3) snap   4) scream   5) attitude
6) condescending   7) behaviors   8) Address   9) busboy   10) horrendous

2. Orally summarize the main ideas of the above passage and write them down on the following lines. (omitted)

Part Three: Watching for Travel 旅游视频

A Complaint in the Restaurant 饭店投诉

Summary:

Complaining about the bad service or food in a restaurant is full of difficulties. Done badly, it could ruin the meal, if the thing you are complaining about hasn't already done so. The help at hand with this easy- to- follow-no-rich-necessary guide to complaining, that even British feel comfortable using.

Step 1: You will need a substandard meal, a slow or rude waiter, a little righteous indignation and a sprinkling of tact.

Step 2: Act immediately. The key to successful complaining is to highlight the problem immediately, thereby giving the restaurant the opportunity to resolve the problem with minimum fuss——don't wait until you've eaten half of an inedible meal or for the bill to arrive to voice an objection.

Step 3: Identify your aims. Think about what you hope to achieve by complaining. Would an apology be enough? Would you like your food replaced? Or do you expect money off the bill? If there is a hygiene issue you are unlikely to want a replacement meal and would probably just like to leave without being charged.

Step 4: What can you expect? Make sure your suggested resolution matches your complaint. If a meal you have ordered is well cooked and served as described on the menu, but you just don't like it, it's unreasonable to demand compensation. However, if you ask politely, many restaurants will be happy to offer you an alternative.

Step 5: Allergies and dislikes. There are often ingredients guides on menus, but to avoid problems it is worth telling the waiter of any allergies or aversions to particular ingredients while you're ordering. If any of the stated ingredients are then present in your meal, you should complain and send it back immediately.

Step 6: Contain your rage. You are less likely to get what you want by being rude or aggressive with a waiter. Discretely call them over, explain the problem, express your disappointment and ask them to resolve the situation.

Step 7: Be assertive. Don't be shy—you're paying for a meal to be cooked properly and to be waited on efficiently and politely. If this isn't your experience, then you are well within your rights to complain.

Step 8: The next level. If your concerns are not met with an acceptable resolution, ask politely to speak to the manager. Explain the problem and state that you are not satisfied with how it has been resolved.

Step 9: Tipping. If service has been poor, reducing the tip or not leaving one at all is a powerful way of expressing your displeasure. However, if the food was of a low standard but the waiter did a good job of addressing your complaint by giving you a discount or complimentary dish, then a tip is still appropriate.

Step 10: Outside help. If after complaining to the waiter and the manager, you still feel like you have been fobbed off, it's time to take your complaints to a higher authority. Contact your local consumer standards body for advice. In the UK you can try the Citizens Advice Bureau or the Office of Fair Trading.

Step 11: Illness. If once you've left a restaurant you become ill from food poisoning that you believe can be traced back to the restaurant, you should immediately report it to the food standards agency or department of health for everyone else's benefit as well as your own.

Step 12: Compliment. As important as it is to complain if something has gone wrong during a meal, it's equally important to compliment and reward good or exceptional service. Whether it's good or bad, feedback is often appreciated by managers as it offers them a real insight to the service they are providing, so speak up and enjoy your meal.

Part Four: Reading for Travel 旅游阅读

Customer Service 客户服务

1. Survey: Take this fun quiz to find out if you can offer good services to the customers.

Reference Keys 参考答案

1) T	2) T	3) F	4) F	5) T
6) F	7) F	8) T	9) T	10) F

2. Discuss: Can you make a good service person? (omitted)

Part Five: Writing for Travel 旅游写作

A letter of complaints 投诉信

Read the following letter and write a letter of complaints in which you lodge a claim on the travel agency for the poor guiding service. (omitted)

Part Six: Singing for Travel 旅游歌曲

Hey Jude 嘿，朱迪
The Beatles

1. Singing English songs together with tourists can stimulate their interest, and liven up the atmosphere when they travel. Listen to the song casually with reference to the lyrics. (omitted)

2. One student role plays a tour guide while others act as tourists. Sing and enjoy the English song together. (omitted)

Part Seven: Additional Know-how 知识扩展

Make a Wise and Polite Complaint 有礼有节地投诉

Read the passage aloud, and decide whether the following statements are true or false. Write T for true and F for false.

1) F	2) T	3) T	4) T	5) F

References
参考文献

[1] 朱华. 英语导游听说教程(修订版)[M]. 北京：北京大学出版社，2008.
[2] 朱华. 英语导游实务教程[M]. 2版. 北京：北京大学出版社，2009.
[3] 朱华，朱红. 旅游英语视听说[M]. 北京：北京大学出版社，2011.
[4] 周玮，钱中丽，周爱洁. 旅游英语应用文[M]. 广州：广东旅游出版社，2000.

北京大学出版社本科旅游管理系列规划教材

序号	书　名	标准书号	主编	定价	出版时间	配套情况
1	旅游学	7-301-22518-9	李瑞	30	2013	课件
2	旅游学概论	7-301-21610-1	李玉华	42	2013	课件
3	旅游学导论	7-301-21325-4	张金霞	36	2012	课件
4	旅游心理学	7-301-23475-4	杨娇	41	2014	课件
5	旅游策划理论与实务	7-301-22630-8	李锋 李萌	43	2013	课件
6	景区经营与管理	7-301-23364-1	陈玉英	48	2013	课件
7	旅游资源开发与规划	7-301-22451-9	孟爱云	32	2013	课件
8	旅游规划原理与实务	7-301-21221-9	郭伟	35	2012	课件
9	旅游地图编制与应用	7-301-23104-3	凌善金	38	2013	课件
10	旅游地形象设计学	7-301-20946-2	凌善金	30	2012	课件
11	旅游英语	7-301-23087-9	朱华	48	2014	课件
12	旅游英语教程	7-301-22042-9	于立新	38	2013	课件
13	英语导游实务	7-301-22986-6	唐勇	33	2013	课件
14	导游实务	7-301-22045-0	易婷婷	29	2013	课件
15	导游实务	7-301-21638-5	朱斌	32	2013	课件
16	旅游文化与传播	7-301-19349-5	潘文焰	38	2012	课件
17	旅游服务礼仪	7-301-22940-8	徐兆寿	29	2013	课件
18	休闲学导论	7-301-22654-4	李经龙	30	2013	课件
19	休闲学导论	7-301-21655-2	吴文新	49	2013	课件
20	休闲活动策划与服务	7-301-22113-6	杨梅	32	2013	课件
21	旅游财务会计	7-301-20101-5	金莉芝	40	2012	课件
22	前厅客房服务与管理	7-301-22547-9	张青云	42	2013	课件
23	现代酒店管理与服务案例	7-301-17449-4	邢夫敏	29	2012	课件
24	餐饮运行与管理	7-301-21049-9	单铭磊	39	2012	课件
25	会展概论	7-301-21091-8	来逢波	33	2012	课件
26	旅行社门市管理实务	7-301-19339-6	梁雪松	39	2011	课件
27	餐饮经营管理	7-5038-5792-8	孙丽坤	30	2010	课件
28	现代旅行社管理	7-5038-5458-3	蒋长春	34	2010	课件
29	旅游学基础教程	7-5038-5363-0	王明星	43	2009	课件
30	民俗旅游学概论	7-5038-5373-9	梁福兴	34	2009	课件
31	旅游资源学	7-5038-5375-3	郑耀星	28	2009	课件
32	旅游信息系统	7-5038-5344-9	夏琛珍	18	2009	课件
33	旅游景观美学	7-5038-5345-6	祁颖	22	2009	课件
34	前厅客房服务与管理	7-5038-5374-6	王华	34	2009	课件
35	旅游市场营销学	7-5038-5443-9	程道品	30	2009	课件
36	中国人文旅游资源概论	7-5038-5601-3	朱桂凤	26	2009	课件
37	观光农业概论	7-5038-5661-7	潘贤丽	22	2009	课件
38	饭店管理概论	7-5038-4996-1	张利民	35	2008	课件
39	现代饭店管理	7-5038-5283-1	尹华光	36	2008	课件
40	旅游策划理论与实务	7-5038-5000-4	王衍用	20	2008	课件
41	中国旅游地理	7-5038-5006-6	周凤杰	28	2008	课件
42	旅游摄影	7-5038-5047-9	夏峰	36	2008	
43	酒店人力资源管理	7-5038-5030-1	张玉改	28	2008	课件
44	旅游服务礼仪	7-5038-5040-0	胡碧芳	23	2008	课件
45	旅游经济学	7-5038-5036-3	王梓	28	2008	课件
46	旅游文化学概论	7-5038-5008-0	曹诗图	23	2008	课件
47	旅游企业财务管理	7-5038-5302-9	周桂芳	32	2008	课件
48	旅游心理学	7-5038-5293-0	邹本涛	32	2008	课件
49	旅游政策与法规	7-5038-5306-7	袁正新	37	2008	课件
50	野外旅游探险考察教程	7-5038-5384-5	崔铁成	31	2008	课件

相关教学资源如电子课件、电子教材、习题答案等可登录 www.pup6.com 下载或在线阅读。

扑六知识网(www.pup6.com)有海量的相关教学资源和电子教材供阅读及下载(包括北京大学出版社第六事业部的相关资源)，同时欢迎您将教学课件、视频、教案、素材、习题、试卷、辅导材料、课改成果、设计作品、论文等教学资源上传到 pup6.com，与全国高校师生分享您的教学成就与经验，并可自由设定价格，知识也能创造财富。具体情况请登录网站查询。

如您需要免费纸质样书用于教学，欢迎登陆第六事业部门户网(www.pup6.com)填表申请，并欢迎在线登记选题以到北京大学出版社来出版您的大作，也可下载相关表格填写后发到我们的邮箱，我们将及时与您取得联系并做好全方位的服务。

扑六知识网将打造成全国最大的教育资源共享平台，欢迎您的加入——让知识有价值，让教学无界限，让学习更轻松。

联系方式：010-62750667，moyu333333@163.com，lihu80@163.com，欢迎来电来信。